"Pot" and what every parent and teenager should know about it.

Estimates reveal that as many as 10 million people in the United States are now using marijuana on a regular basis. The use of "grass" or "pot" is now so widespread that there are now movements afoot to legalize the use of marijuana, thus paving the way for machine-packaged marijuana by leading tobacco companies. An experienced counselor in the drug world, Don Wilkerson now reveals the often-ignored dangers of a marijuana habit, and speaks to young and old alike regarding the solution for this, America's fastest growing drug problem. Find out the hidden facts about this drug, and how to deal with it effectively and definitely.

SHOCKING NEW FACTS ABOUT MARIJUANA

Don Wilkerson

SPIRE BOOKS

Fleming H. Revell Company
Old Tappan, New Jersey

Contents

1 Legalized Pot?   11
2 Reefer Madness   23
3 The Colombian Connection   39
4 Grass Roots   49
5 The Medical Case Against Marijuana   63
6 Decriminalization—Blessing or Curse?   79
7 How to Guard Kids Against Drugs   95
8 The Courage to Say "No"   113

SHOCKING NEW FACTS ABOUT

MARIJUANA

1

Legalized Pot?

TEENAGERS PAY TO HAVE FATHER KILLED. The story behind this headline is that of two Cleveland, Ohio, teenagers who paid another youth $60 to kill their father. The forty-one-year-old man was shot in the head with a .38 caliber handgun. According to the police, the two children then proceeded to go through their dad's pockets, took his $230 paycheck plus some $60 in cash, and went on a ten-day spending spree, acquiring, among other things, a television set and various games.

When the fourteen-year-old girl and seventeen-year-old boy were asked why they did it, they answered, "Because he wouldn't let us do anything we wanted to do, like smoke pot."

Marijuana—pot, tea, hash, reefer, grass—is the number-one drug of choice among American youth. While killing for it, as in the above story, is an extreme and bizarre result of marijuana smoking, nevertheless millions of teenagers and young adults are endangering their lungs, brains, reproductive organs, and their lives and those of others by the habitual abuse of smoking brown grass rolled into home-made-type cigarettes.

The National Institute of Drug Abuse (NIDA) reported

that in 1977, 28 percent of youngsters between the ages of
12 and 17 reported having used marijuana. Four percent
of the surveyed 12- to 13-year-olds had smoked marijuana
"during the past month." And one in nine high-school seniors smoked marijuana daily. Teenager use has doubled
since 1965.

The *Seventh Annual Report on Marijuana and Health*,
encompassing a study of the drugs used during 1977, estimated *43 million Americans have tried marijuana at least
once and about 16 million had used it within one month
before the survey*. Comparing this with previous findings,
marijuana use among teenagers is reported to have increased by one-third. *There may be 10 million regular
users*.

Joseph A. Califano, then secretary of health, education,
and welfare, said he was "deeply disturbed" by the upswing
in pot smoking, especially among teenagers, and announced
a redoubling of government research on the effects of its
use. "It is sheer folly for millions of young Americans to
indulge in a drug while so little is known about its long-
term consequences—and when much of what is known sug-
gests, for example, adverse pulmonary effects and psy-
chomotor impairment," Califano stated in a UPI-released
story.

The above-mentioned report on marijuana said a com-
posite portrait of the most frequent pot smoker shows a
college-educated white male, aged twenty-two to twenty-
five, living in the West. But it also said nearly three out
of ten youngsters aged twelve to seventeen have tried marijuana, and one out of six uses it regularly—with a national
survey showing the attitude of the young toward marijuana
is becoming "increasingly positive."

The survey also found that youngsters and young adults do not consider marijuana addictive, but three out of five older than twenty-six do.

The report confirmed what most experts have been saying: Marijuana is so widespread, it is becoming the new alcohol of this era. Not that it is replacing alcohol, for youthful alcohol consumption is also on the rise; it is taking the place of cigarettes among young puffers and inhalers.

Therefore, parents, get ready! Marijuana, machine-packaged by a leading tobacco company, may soon be on its way to your neighborhood store, with the United States Seal of Approval stamped right on it. The move is on—by a well-organized, well-funded lobby—to have Congress pass a new federal marijuana-decriminalization law. This is intended to lead eventually to a total legalization of the drug.

What will this mean to our society?

What will it mean to our children?

How will it affect future generations?

Is it possible to put a stop to this move for marijuana decriminalization and legalization?

What have been the effects of the decriminalization laws already passed and in operation in certain states?

Will marijuana become the new alcohol of the '80s? What are the short- and long-term effects of its use?

These and other questions must be faced now. Dr. Robert L. DuPont, former director of NIDA, stated, in an article by Peggy Mann:

> While Americans are debating the question of criminal penalties for marijuana possession, the real tragedy has overtaken us almost unnoticed. . . . The real danger is the health danger posed by the epi-

demic danger of at least two kinds. One is the effects of the intoxication, ranging from the hazardous impact on driving to caring less about everything. The other area is purely physical. Here the concerns range from the regular occurrence of chronic bronchitis among marijuana smokers to the very real possibility of harmful effects . . . and possible cancer.

Smoking one marijuana joint is the equivalent of smoking one pack of cigarettes. *Five joints (of marijuana) have the same effect as smoking 112 tobacco cigarettes.*

Literally, our youth may be "going up in smoke." In addition to the rise in the use of marijuana, use of cocaine, angel dust, pills, and alcohol is on the increase. An estimated 30 to 40 percent of American teenagers drink alcohol excessively. Approximately one-half million may be alcoholics. Thus, we have a drug combo—pot, booze, and other dangerous narcotics—threatening to take its toll on our children. And it is happening without most parents really knowing its full impact on our youth and society.

I cannot offer much hope to parents in regard to stopping marijuana's decriminalization, given the moral trends in society. Whether through decriminalization of the present laws or full-scale legalization, marijuana is and has become easier and easier to obtain. Marijuana is probably the fastest-growing industry of one South American country (the source of the majority of grass presently being smuggled into this country); therefore, there is a vast supply of the stuff, even without legalization.

School authorities wink at it or act as if they don't want to see what's going on. (One school that had the courage

to search for marijuana by sending in trained dogs to sniff
for it will probably be hit with a lawsuit for invasion of
privacy.)

This public tolerance toward drugs has the law-enforcement people confused. In April 1979, the city of Berkeley,
California, passed legislation requiring the police to make
enforcement of state marijuana laws their "lowest priority."
The law passed by a substantial margin.

Without the moral support and the backing of the community at large, the police lack the necessary incentive to
carry out whatever form of law does exist to keep drugs
away from our youth and keep our schools and youth hang-
outs from being an open marketplace for the sale and distribution of not just pot, but other dangerous narcotics.

In general, there is a new tolerance toward the use of
drugs. Never before has society so changed its mind about
a dangerous (or, at least, a potentially dangerous) drug such
as marijuana. We have gone from a tough stand against it
in the '60s to a tolerance of it in the '70s and the prospect
of its legalization in the '80s. I'll explore a few of the reasons
for this turnabout in the pages that follow.

The key issue, however, is: How will all this affect our
children? Can parents prepare themselves and their children against the possibility of legalized marijuana?

What should parents know about the physical and psychological effects of pot, so they can give their kids factual
reasons why they should not smoke it?

Since we can no longer depend on the government to
protect our children from marijuana and other drugs, as
concerned parents, we must prepare a moral and spiritual

defense against it. As such, it is important to become as knowledgeable about its dangers as possible, yet at the same time not panic or overreact if and when our own teenagers are found to be trying it.

Most of all, we will have to teach our young people how to build inner defense mechanisms and inner controls against the temptation to experiment with marijuana in particular and other artificial "highs" in general. In the final analysis, it is the inner legislation of the heart that acts as the policeman to help us and our kids keep away from forbidden fruit.

What if that fails? What if our children refuse to accept the Christian-Judeo standards that say "keep off the grass"? What if parents discover their teenager to be smoking pot or using some other form of narcotic?

It takes a very mature parent to face this trauma. It is mom's and dad's reaction to drug abuse in the home that is as much a key to getting the teenager to quit as anything else.

The parent can begin by acquiring as much knowledge about drugs as is possible. Neither ignorance nor emotion over our children's pot smoking will help matters. We must face the reality of raising children in the '80s: Drugs, and especially marijuana, are becoming as common as cigarette smoking. Just as all kids—Christian or non-Christian, churchgoing or nonchurchgoing—have to face the drug issue, so all parents must work out a strategy to protect their kids.

I would like to say a word or two about why I have chosen to write this book at this time. I say "at this time" because it would seem that, over the past ten years or so, we have been flooded with materials on the dangers of drugs. When the drug revolution hit middle America in the '60s (previously it was primarily confined to the inner cities and ghettos), we were totally unprepared for it. For a long time it was ignored. Many parents could not believe their children were addicted. The result was a crash program of drug education, put out in the schools and in the communities by both private and government agencies. What good they did, or what effect these programs and materials had on preventing further drug abuse, is suspect. They probably had few positive results. Some people say they had none at all. Others go as far as to say the drug-education programs created more problems by causing young people to become curious about the drugs they were being told were no good for them.

If the publishing of drug materials, lectures, and discussions, and the presenting of educational programs, did anything, it made us aware that there was a problem. And there still is. However, we are less aware of it now than ever, in spite of all the attention on the problem over the past ten to fifteen years. Society now acts as if it doesn't know or doesn't care about the drug problem.

Also, since public attention has been turned aside from drugs—due to our preoccupation with rising inflation, the energy crisis, and other national and international problems—it is time once again to take a closer look at the youth of America and see what they are up to. One thing is for sure: They are "going up in smoke." It is time to wake up. The pro-marijuana organizations are busy at work, influencing the lawmakers to decriminalize the drug. Therefore I say: America, wake up . . . parents, wake up . . . school officials, wake up! Find out what is going on in the drug scene.

We are already a nation of boozers; that is bad enough. Now we are about to add another legalized vice to society. Enough is enough. While we may not be able to stop the moral landslide completely, we can at least let our kids know our opposition to it. I can't change the alcohol laws in our country, but I can preach and promote a moral stand against its use and abuse, which will enlist voluntary abstinence. I believe we can do the same in respect to the use and abuse of marijuana.

This does not mean I believe we should give up trying to prevent its legalization or that we cannot pressure our schools and police to continue to enforce the present laws against its use. We can. I admire what one community in Indiana had the courage to do. The police, in cooperation with the high-school authorities, conducted a room-by-room search for drugs, using trained German shepherds and Doberman pinschers in the surprise raid. A controversy followed the action, when the American Civil Liberties Union threatened to bring a lawsuit against the police and school officials. They claimed the civil rights of the 2,780 students were violated.

A group of parents then rose up in support of the school administration. "The schools have been pussyfooting around for years and not doing anything about the drug problem, and I fully support the raids," said one father who had a child in the school. "I have no concern about the students' rights being violated," he said. "Why should my kids have to be exposed to drugs?"

Another mother, with one child in the junior high school

and another in elementary school, commented, "If the ACLU wins, drugs will flow like water in Indiana. Fear, tempered with respect, like the fear of God, will help the children avoid a tragedy like drugs."

Unless and until the federal government is willing to resist the decriminalization-campaign pressure groups and local communities let school authorities know they want drug abuse curbed, more and more of our kids will be challenged to toke on a joint.

At present, I categorize four different types of marijuana users:

1. **The abuser** Usually this young person is searching for anything to get high and/or escape from life. This is the mixed-up, lonely, emotionally starved youth—often the victim of a poor home environment. Rebellion and bitterness may also motivate the abuse of drugs. He (or she) uses marijuana, and often other drugs, to act out and get even with parents or society for the bad deal he feels he has been dealt. Pot smoking in this case is only the symptom of a much deeper need and problem.

Among the abusers is the "don't confuse me with the facts, my mind is already made up" type. No matter how many times they are warned or what harm they see drugs doing to others, they have a *need* to get high. In fact, for some, the more dangerous, bizarre, or risky the drug trip, the more they will respond.

The abuser needs special attention and counsel and perhaps a Christian rehabilitation program. Many have to hit rock bottom or get worse before they will get better and admit they need help and submit to those who can help.

2. **The user**   Millions now smoke pot in the same manner and for the same reasons people drink—for its pleasure and a temporary high. These are the recreational users. Just as many teens and adults view sex as a mere pleasure to be indulged in at will (called recreational sex), so it follows that pot is smoked with the same promiscuous motivation and attitude. These include the "weekender," the "party smoker," and the "event smoker" (such as those who attend rock concerts or sporting events as an excuse to enjoy pot). Marijuana is more and more replacing tobacco as the smoker's weed choice.

Dr. Edward R. Bloomquist, in his excellent book *Marijuana: The Second Trip*, identifies three types of users:

> Antisocial misfits, the "lower-caste" group (i.e. uneducated and usually unemployed and poorly motivated), who have from the beginning used the drug as an added chorus to an already established refrain of antiauthoritarianism, antidisciplinarianism, and antisocial activities.
>
> The "upper caste" . . . who is far more interested in the use of the drug for self-exploration, mind expansion, and socio-relaxation. . . . In addition to committed users, we find the intellectuals, pseudointellectuals, and religious and pseudoreligious people. This group tends to pursue a search for inner truth and inner peace.
>
> The third group is the largest. It is composed primarily of average, curious, uninhibited people out for a lark. These youngsters are usually "chippers," that is, they play with the drug now and then as the mood directs them.

3. **The "straight" kid** This is the young person who does not use drugs, because he or she has no need or desire for it. This is the committed youngster. The commitment may be to God, to church, to acquiring an education, to boyfriend or girl friend, marriage, or any other worthwhile goal. This is the child who is often motivated by spiritual and moral principles and whose needs are thus being met by the legitimate and natural (or supernatural) blessings of life. This young person usually does not have to worry about the temptation to use drugs, because he or she is so stimulated and turned-on by such a commitment and to following the straight and narrow way.

4. **The undecided** This "in-betweener," representing the largest group, has to fight tremendous peer pressure and the philosophy that "everyone's doing it." As with any youth fad or practice, to not go along with the crowd is to be made to feel guilty by the users and abusers. The undecided youth feels caught between the need to be popular and accepted by peers and the responsibility to obey parents and/or God. This is the youngster who concerns me. He is the reason schools, churches, parents, and community organizations must develop counter-peer-pressure groups, to help the morally and spiritually weakening youth resist the seductive pressure of his friends and schoolmates.

This also *may* be the youngster who has all the outward appearances of being okay but is quietly and secretly smoking a joint at a party or dance or being turned on by a friend. Most users and abusers are not introduced to drugs (especially marijuana) by some sleazy-looking street pusher, but by a known or even trusted friend.

The undecided youth who does give in to the users can

be reached if something is done soon enough, especially before the initial guilt wears off and the youth culture makes him feel his habit is no big deal.

It is with this type of child and teenager in mind that this material is being prepared for parents, counselors, and all who are concerned about the pressures our youth are under in schools and in their communities. To smoke or not to smoke is one of those pressures. I hope both adult and teenager will find good advice in the pages that follow. Proverbs 10:8 (TEV) says, "Sensible people accept good advice. . . ." Given the right information, many of our youth are capable and willing to make the right decisions regarding pot smoking.

And given the right spiritual perspective on life, they can become sensible people, ready to accept good advice. I agree 100 percent with the mother quoted above: "Fear, tempered with respect, like the fear of God, will help the children avoid a tragedy like drugs."

2

Reefer Madness

SOME MAY WONDER why all the whoopla about pot. Why the controversy surrounding it? What has caused the emotionally charged debate around this strange weed? What is "reefer madness"?

In 1935, a low-budget film called *Reefer Madness* portrayed the so-called evils of marijuana. It declared that pot smoking led to murder, rape, suicide, and other similar evils. Today the movie has become a pot-culture feature, shown in thousands of college theaters and movie houses—as well as at pot parties—as a parody of the falsehoods and paranoia that once surrounded the use of marijuana.

Why the paranoia? Where did it originate?

A brief history of *Cannabis sativa* (Latin for "canelike" and "cultivated"), the hemp plant from which the marijuana weed is produced, provides some insight on how reefer madness originated. The earliest writings referring to *Cannabis sativa* date as far back as 2700–2500 B.C. According to *The Marijuana Catalog,* "Credit for the first use of marijuana should probably go to the nomadic people of the Central Asian plains, who spread the weed through China and later to India. By 2500 B.C. Indian culture was full of religious songs and hymns praising the use of *soma*, which by all indications was *Cannabis*."

Marijuana's entrance into the western culture was in the 1900s, when the plant was widely grown in Virginia, presumably for its fiber, which was used to make rope. It is reported that George Washington grew it as a cash crop because of its fiber use. *The Marijuana Catalog* states: "It was no more regarded as a plant drug than the Morning Glory."

Also, in the mid-1800s the plant appeared in a new form, as a medicine for a wide variety of ailments, and was listed in drug-reference manuals of that time. The extract of hemp was reportedly used in treating such ailments as gout, rheumatism, epidemic cholera, and other things. In Poland, Russia, and Lithuania, hemp was used to treat toothaches by inhaling the vapor from seeds thrown into hot stones. Larry Sloman observes, in *Reefer Madness:*

> In New York City during the 1920's, it was not uncommon for Russian and Polish immigrants to trek over to Nassau Street, buy bulk Cannabis, return to their Lower East Side tenements, throw the Cannabis on the radiator, using a towel to form a smoke chamber, and inhale the fumes for respiratory ailments.

> As a medicinal agent, marijuana generally fell into disfavor before the turn of the century. For one, it was insoluble and therefore could not be injected, so there were delays of three hours when administered orally. Secondly, there was tremendous difficulty in standardizing the dosage, as different batches showed variations in potency. Also, there were variations

among individuals in their response to the drug. So, when the new synthetic drugs were introduced—drugs which, like morphine, were capable of administration by the newly discovered hypodermic syringe—Cannabis use decreased.

However, as a recreational drug, Cannabis was just beginning to be discovered by adventurous Americans.

In the '20s, jazz vocalists were singing about the elusive "reefer man," and by the '30s, marijuana continued to be popular among jazz musicians and immigrants from Jamaica and the West Indies, where it was quite prevalent and where they learned to acquire a taste for it. For them, it was a part of their life-style, but in America, they stayed outside the mainstream of society, and so did marijuana.

It was also in the '20s that marijuana—as at that time it first came to be described when taken for nonmedical purposes—began to acquire a sinister reputation. This was due in part to the stories coming out of Egypt, where hashish was still being blamed for the high addiction rate. At the same time, the use of marijuana began to spread from the South (where it had been used primarily by slaves) to the North—into states of the Union where it had not been known before.

At about the same time, the Federal Bureau of Narcotics was established as a wing of the Treasury Department in Washington, D.C. (1930). It moved to have marijuana banned throughout the country. The Treasury Department would not go along with this and issued the following statement:

A great deal of public interest has been aroused by newspaper articles appearing from time to time on the evils of the abuse of marijuana, or Indian hemp. This publicity tends to magnify the extent of the evil and lends color to the inference that there is an alarming spread of the improper use of the drug, whereas the actual increase in such use may not have been inordinately large.

Harry Anslinger, first chief of the new narcotics bureau, set out to make the smoking of marijuana a crime of high degree. He was disturbed at the Treasury Department for rejecting his efforts to ban it, and when given the power of his new position, he endeavored to use it to get Congress to rule in his favor. Anslinger had been assistant commissioner for Prohibition. According to *The Forbidden Game,* he had a "deep repugnance for drugs dating back, by his own account, to an episode in his childhood. He had been born in Pennsylvania near a township in which one adult out of ten was reported to be an opium addict. And as a twelve-year-old, he heard a woman screaming in agony for the drug, a sound he never forgot. He had come to feel the same horror of marijuana." Anslinger's bureau was successful, and in 1937 the Treasury Department introduced a federal marijuana bill, putting the drug into the same category as the hard narcotics controlled by the Harrison Act. Prior to, and immediately following, the passage of the new marijuana law, a flood of materials in the form of pamphlets, booklets, radio broadcasts, and lectures was produced, either directly by Anslinger or by his directive. The bureau chief realized that he had to do a better job of controlling the drug than he had been able to do with alcohol. One of the people Anslinger turned to to aid his campaign against marijuana was a "hot-gospeller" by the name of Earl Albert Rowell; who had been touring America lecturing audiences on marijuana's effect.

The drug, according to Rowell's estimations, was evil for the following reasons:

1. Destroys willpower, making a jellyfish of the user. He cannot say no.
2. Eliminates the line between right and wrong.
3. Above all, causes crime, fills the victim with an irrepressible urge to violence.
4. Incites to revolting immorality, including rape and murder.
5. Causes many accidents, both industrial and automotive.
6. Ruins careers forever.
7. Causes insanity as its specialty.
8. Either in self-defense or as a means of revenue, users make smokers of others, thus perpetuating evil.

However, when Rowell tried to link cigarette smoking to pot, Anslinger had to back off. Rowell tried to show cigarette smoking was a stepping-stone to the use of marijuana.

I cite the above bit of history to show how and why marijuana has been so surrounded by controversy. The confusion is further demonstrated by the wide variance among the states on the penalties for possession and use of marijuana. The laws also reveal that those who sought to link marijuana with heroin and other dangerous drugs succeeded. For example, in Alabama, a second conviction for any possession of grass can bring up to 40 years in prison and a $25,000 fine. In Arizona, where at one time possession of one ounce of marijuana could get you life imprisonment, the law now calls for possession of any amount of grass to be prosecuted as a felony. At the same time, the exact same amount resulted in a $20 fine in the state of South Dakota.

In spite of this, it became obvious by the '60s that the campaign to stamp out marijuana was not succeeding. After it surfaced among the beat generation of the '50s and the hippies of the '60s, the habit spread rapidly throughout the country. Until recently, its control was primarily by law enforcement. In 1960, there were 169 arrests in connection with marijuana in the state of Connecticut, but by 1965 there were 7,000 arrests, and in 1966, as its middle-class use spread, there were 15,000 arrests.

In the '70s, public attention began changing toward marijuana and drugs in general, in part due to the vast number of users. The police were willing enough to make raids in hippy camps, but did not relish the idea of making sweeps through the massed ranks of fans at pop festivals. Even less appealing was raiding homes of the GIs—sometimes officers—who had brought the habit back with them from Vietnam.

Politicians, too, could no longer be sure that a hard line on drugs would win them electoral support. In the winter of 1972, the Consumers' Union pronounced "marijuana is here to stay. No conceivable law enforcement can curb its availability."

In 1973, Oregon took a tentative step toward legislation by converting possession of small quantities of marijuana into a violation comparable to a parking offense. While other states have not gone so far in softening their marijuana laws, many have liberalized them.

The proponents and promoters for decriminalized and legalized marijuana are using what I call "reefer madness" to their advantage. There has been a slow, subtle, effective campaign—both organized and unorganized—over the past ten years, taking advantage of the controversy surrounding marijuana's confusing laws, medical findings, and unrealistic efforts to stamp it out. The goal is to dupe the American public into accepting marijuana as a harmless recreational drug.

One thing the marijuana campaigners have used effectively to promote their cause is the media. Just as the news media were used effectively during the '40s, '50s, and '60s to feed the public both factual and inaccurate information about drugs, so now marijuana's Madison Avenue-type promoters are using the media to counteract past inaccuracies. In addition, they have also managed to pull off a cover-up of sorts regarding the most recent findings on its dangers. Thus, marijuana proponents have had a favorable press, while the research and warnings against it have either gone unprinted or been hidden in the back pages of the newspaper.

For example, when television star Mary Tyler Moore made an offhand remark in which she stated, "I've tried marijuana and consider it to be less harmful than alcohol," her picture and statement made front-page news. The result: Millions of kids read it with pleasure. Those looking for reasons they should not worry about its harm are thereby reinforced in their prejudices. And Ms. Moore is made to look like an authority after a few puffs on pot. Later the same evening, Johnny Carson, of the NBC *Tonight* show, made a point to call attention to her pro-pot remark with a smile on his face, as if to say if good and wholesome Mary Tyler Moore smokes pot, it must not be all that bad. But when a doctor or medical-research team uncovers data that indicates marijuana to be harmful to the body, it is unlikely to make either the front or back page of the same paper. One must discover it in a medical journal.

Public apathy and public opinion have turned pro-marijuana, and the media have responded accordingly. The opinion makers and the people who influence and finance them have also joined the ranks of the pot experimenters—and some have become regular users. Maxine Cheshire, in an article in *Family Circle* entitled "Drugs in Washington, D.C." asks the question: "Do pot, cocaine and more dangerous drugs influence our highest decision makers and those close to them?" The article goes on to state:

> In 1978, the social winds continue to blow eastward. Hollywood, bored with alcohol and publicized affairs, has embraced a new high—drugs—and Washington, D.C. is following suit. Many Washington parties serve cocaine and marijuana as naturally as martinis, and insiders suggest that if the total extent of drug abuse in the Capital was exposed, the resulting scandal would touch every area of government—from the hallowed walls of Congress to many a chande-

liered embassy, and even to the White House. Drugs, particularly the "fashionable ones," have become so acceptable in Washington that even some White House guests feel free to indulge in them on the premises.

At the White House's first jazz festival on the South Lawn this summer [1978], a haze of marijuana smoke hung heavy under the low-bending branches of a magnolia tree when President Carter darted behind the bandstand to congratulate the musicians. One of the President's bodyguard looked uncomfortable and feebly fanned the air around his boss. But if Carter recognized the aroma that enveloped him, he pretended to notice nothing.

I have been working in the drug-abuse field for over twenty years. I have watched drug use go from the drug-pusher's house to the White House. Fifteen years ago, I and millions of others would never have believed the above-mentioned report.

In the '60s, drug use was confined to the ghettos and among blacks, Puerto Ricans, Chicanos, and other minority groups. Prior to this period, marijuana was the exclusive indulgence of jazz musicians. It surfaced with the beat generation of the '50s, among poets, artists, and folk musicians. By the late '60s, pot became a new generation's protest drug. A drug revolution spread like wildfire across the country. Kids who previously were protected or isolated from the drug scene were "turning on" and "tuning in."

Paul Dennis and Carolyn Berry, writing in their book *The Marijuana Catalog*, stated:

Marijuana appealed to their [the '60s generation] sense of life's possibilities and helped unify the generation widely diverse in its opinions and interests. The use of marijuana—a sort of "exclusive" habit—gave the new generation a sense of community and shared values. Even the way it was smoked, passed around in a circle, symbolized the communal experience.

From pot, middle- and upper-class students began popping pills, dropping acid, LSD, speed, and other hallucinogenic drugs—even mainlining heroin. And a previously apathetic society was shaken to its WASPy core. When it was the blacks, Hispanic Americans, and minorities abusing drugs, the rest of the country didn't care. But when it broke out in middle America, drug raids in high schools and colleges were common. Every major newspaper and national magazine carried exposés on the drug scene. Taxpayers clamored for the federal, state, and local governments to do something. Drug-treatment and prevention organizations launched a multitude of programs, spending the millions of dollars legislators began to allot for controlling the epidemic of narcotic abuse and addiction. America was on an antidrug and antimarijuana bandwagon.

That has all changed now. It was only a short time after the earlier-mentioned White House jazz festival that Special Assistant to the President for Health Issues, Dr. Peter G. Bourne, resigned when it was alleged he was using recreational drugs (which he denied).

Following the incident, President Carter issued a warning to White House staff workers that he expected everyone to obey the law and anyone using drugs illegally would be fired. "Whether you agree with the law or not is totally irrelevant. . . . you will obey it, or you will seek employment elsewhere."

Maxine Cheshire, in her article "Drugs in Washington, D.C." stated: "The sad truth is that drugs, on the Washington social scene are 'in'. They are trendy, kicky, chic."

What brought about this change in the middle- and upper-class attitude toward drugs? Why have we, within a relatively short time, gone from an anti-pot society to pro-pot? Why have the *bad guys* of the '60s become the *in guys* of the '70s and '80s? Why has the call gone from "lock 'em up" to "let 'em alone"?

I propose there are a number of reasons for this about-face in our drug attitudes:

1. Past efforts to warn kids about drugs contained too many myths, half-truths, and false information.   Marijuana, for example, was lumped in among all the rest of the dangerous drugs. Pot was thought to be a lead-in or stepping-stone to other more potent and dangerous drugs, and it was the beginning drug for the hard-core users in the late '50s and early '60s. Marijuana was, at the time, part and parcel of the whole gamut of narcotics available on the streets. The route from grass to junk was short, easy, and inevitable. Marijuana and heroin were rarely used exclusively of each other.

But then something happened to separate marijuana and the other soft drugs from the hard ones. Speed, LSD, STP, pills, and heroin became the experimental drugs of the middle class in the early '70s. Many became hooked—hard-core junkies. They were no different from the Harlem or ghetto street junkies. This shook our nation to its core. A massive drug-education campaign swept the country. Kids realized, in time, that the hard stuff was a monkey on their backs that they could not get rid of. Adults did all they could to deter all drug use. But in the zeal and desperation to turn kids away from dope, marijuana was lumped in with all drugs. But the users knew differently. Drug use became more sophisticated. Young people learned—some the hard way—that heroin was physically addicting, but marijuana was not. Thus, many drug-education and prevention programs lost credibility with the kids. Young people smoked pot either out of protest or because they knew it was safer than the hallucinogenics and heroin. Marijuana, among middle-class youth, became primarily a recreational drug, while in the poorer areas it continued to be the lead-in drug to the more dangerous stuff.

2. **Marijuana became the "lesser evil by comparison" drug.** Because all the attention was focused on preventing, controlling, and treating the hard-core users, and because the myths surrounding marijuana were finally exposed, it ended up the drug of choice of the majority of young people who wanted to experiment with drugs but not go to the extent of the street junkie. "Pot is not addicting," the kids would say in justification or defense of their smoking grass. "It's no worse than alcohol," was and is the other popular argument. Therefore I believe marijuana has won popularity by default. It has sneaked in, so to speak, while the country was worrying about and chasing the pusher and heroin junkies. Unfortunately, while liberalizing marijuana laws because of this "lesser evil by comparison" method, no one was examining the dangers of marijuana on its own merits. Naturally, marijuana comes

out the innocent party when compared with LSD, speed, heroin, and other types of hard drugs. But marijuana needs no comparison. It is a drug. It must be analyzed on its own. Why we have allowed the proponents of marijuana to launch their campaign to decriminalize it without challenge or investigation into its prolonged effects on regular users is a mystery. The idea that marijuana is harmless is a great American hoax.

3. **Drugs have reached the upper crust.** From Hollywood to Washington, D.C., pot (and now cocaine) is becoming as common as booze and broken marriages. Or, as another stated, drugs are consumed as freely as hors d'oeuvres.

"It's not possible to have a party without someone using drugs," says one hostess.

In fact, pot smoking among stars and upper-class professionals is so common in some places that it's not even given a second thought. Many celebrities are turning on with "coke" (cocaine) for various reasons. In addition to using it as a party pleasure, some are using it during work—even taking it before a game show or talk program, claiming it intensifies their reactions and kills on-camera jitters. Mike Douglas claims that some of his guest stars come on the program stoned.

Jan Goodwin, writing in *Family Circle* magazine, asks the question, "Can drugs affect government decisions?" She further writes:

> The broad social effect of drug-taking by performers and theatrical celebrities can best be measured in the permissive climate it creates and the example

it sets for young people. But when officials at government level are involved, a whole new set of questions arises. Are important decisions being clouded by "recreational" chemicals? Are governments endorsing drug use by "looking the other way?" Is illegality the only reason for disciplining elected public officials and government employees who are known to be drug users?

What is most disturbing about the celebrity drug users is the influence they have over youthful fans. They become very poor models. Couple this with a few key Washington officials, either outrightly condoning marijuana use or giving *tacit* approval of it, and no wonder upwards to 20 percent of the American population is "going up in smoke."

4. **America has lost the war on drugs.** We've lost the war on drugs because we've lost the will to fight against them anymore. Other problems are draining the energy and the pocketbooks of the taxpayers. In addition, the failure of most of the past rehabilitation programs has turned the public away from its previously declared war on narcotics.

History bears out that when our nation cannot control the vices of the citizenry, we end up legalizing our habits in order to get the tax dollar out of them. We are very near doing this with marijuana. Technically, we have not legalized heroin, but the government has thrown in the towel, in effect, in trying to rehabilitate hard-core addicts. The number-one drug pushers in America are the federal and state government drug agencies that dispense methadone. They thus end up perpetuating the addicts' addiction.

"We must accept the fact that heroin addicts have a

disease. We must give them methadone in the same manner that diabetics must take insulin," one official stated. Drug abuse no longer stirs the emotions of Americans as it once did. We have come to believe that drugs, especially marijuana, are like alcohol—that they're here to stay. Some of the very same people who in past days stood up against the abuse of drugs now condone marijuana, embrace it, and smoke it.

One thing has also changed in the drug itself. Colombian-cultivated marijuana is now the prevailing street-level pot in use. It is stronger, on an average, by ten times than the marijuana that had been available over the past years. This is why the air and seaways are crowded with new-time smugglers, taking advantage not only of official and unofficial tolerance toward marijuana smoking, but cashing in on the more potent quality of the Colombian hemp plant.

3

The Colombian Connection

A United States customs agent called me from his office in Chicago to ask if I thought any of the young men in Teen Challenge—former drug addicts—might be able to provide his agency with information that might help them track down some drug pushers. He hoped to obtain information relative to a drug-smuggling ring. I was not able to help him.

The government agencies responsible for trying to stop the flow of marijuana, cocaine, and other drugs into the United States do need help; that is without doubt. "We are intercepting very little of the drugs coming in," the customs agent told me. Daily, 130,000 pounds of marijuana makes its way into the lungs of an estimated 42 million Americans who have tried pot. Annually, 25 billion dollars is spent on joints. Eighty percent of the marijuana comes from Colombia, which is to the pot smuggler what the French Connection has been to the heroin trafficker. Illegal drugs are becoming the biggest worldwide industry. The combined total of all Colombian smuggling profits now approaches $3 billion per year—$700 million more than all of that country's legal exports. Some prominent Colombian figures are even suggesting that the incredibly profitable drug market might well be institutionalized in the near future.

Colombia is an ideal country for growing marijuana, known there as Santa Marta gold. Because of favorable soil conditions, an ideal Andes climate, and an ideal shoreline of regular terrain, this part of South America is the marijuana grower's paradise. There are approximately 250,000 acres of cultivated land available for growing the plant. It has made this small South American country the world's drug provider.

Peter Bensinger, head of the United States Drug Enforcement Administration, says: "It's a trafficker's paradise. Colombia is the largest supplier of marijuana in the world."

The Colombian fields have a potential of producing 6 billion pounds of marijuana annually. Each pound is worth an estimated $600 on the American streets. With this vast supply, it is no wonder that ships, planes, and commercial air travelers have established smuggling routes from Bogota to New York, Chicago, and Los Angeles. In between the 5000 miles is a network of farmers, smugglers, brokers, and fixers—all getting a cut of the action.

With such high profits at stake, it is no surprise that so many novices and small-time entrepreneurs are risking their efforts to cash in on such a growth industry. A June 17, 1974, *New York Times* article, entitled INVESTIGATORS SAY EL PASO [Texas] IS NOW A MAJOR HUB FOR DRUG TRAFFICKING, quotes a special agent of the FBI, who stated, "Some of the community's most upright citizens, including 'doctors, lawyers, and businessmen,' were providing seed money for narcotics smuggling. Many of these 'good, solid citizens,' Mr. Dobbs went on, "were attracted to the business by the rate of return, as high as 25 percent a week, but others were victims of extortion through prostitution."

A 1979 murder of District Judge John H. Wood, Jr.—the first federal judge to be murdered in more than a century—is believed to have been the result of his hard line against convicted drug smugglers. The *New York Times* called Judge Wood "a merciless enemy of drug traffickers. He assessed the maximum legal penalty in 72 of his 90 narcotics cases that ended in convictions."

Since 1974, marijuana consumption has quadrupled, which is no doubt the reason for the rush to cash in on the lucrative market. *Time* magazine, in its January 29, 1979, issue, stated, "The big money in the Colombian drug operation goes not to those who grow narcotics or process it, but to those who get them to the American consumer. One way to get the drug out is to supply them from one of the hundreds of clandestine airstrips that have been bulldozed in the Guajira Peninsula."

There are an estimated 800 airstrips on the Guajira Peninsula of Colombia. There may be as many in Florida. Some landings are done between the headlight beams of two pickup trucks on secluded, flat land, thus avoiding radar detection and making it difficult for investigators to detect.

One daredevil pilot, who has made nearly 130 runs, stated in an interview in the January, 1979, issue of *High Times* magazine: "The pot lanes are busier than the commercial routes over Palm Beach Airport. I've seen MAF planes lined up for hours waiting to land. The situation is really getting dangerous. There have probably been mid-air collisions."

He was asked, "How much do you make?"

"About $10 a pound. . . . There is no Mr. Big. If you take 6,000 pounds, there's probably 600 people involved in it by the time it gets down to the street."

With the possibility of making $25,000 to $50,000 in a 24-hour period, it is no wonder pilots are in plenty. This is, of course, all tax free. Some pilots and planes have been lost at sea—with the rush to cash in on the lucrative business, poorly serviced engines and marginally safe planes are not uncommon—yet the high pay out spurs the smuggler on, in spite of such risks. The Colombian military reportedly seize a drug-laden craft per day, but even this does not keep the sky smuggler grounded. Some pilots are even unlicensed.

How effective are the United States' efforts to stop such pilots or other types of smugglers? *Time* magazine quoted Coast Guard Admiral John Hayes, who said, "We are at almost a wartime status, but we are intercepting only about 10 percent of the illegal drugs coming in."

Time says, "Successful smugglers hardly bother to hide their activities."

A sister industry—airplane brokering—has also sprung up, as a result of the large numbers involved in the smuggling. The brokers—they usually are not involved in the drug trafficking, but occasionally may be—provide the smugglers with a lease and lend wings, equipped with the extra fuel tank necessary for making the long flight back and forth across the Caribbean. Fake corporate documents often make it impossible for the authorities to trace the ownership, or even the identity, of the aircraft.

"There have been times when we had the airplane and the dope physically in our hands and were not able to find out who owned it," said an agent of the Federal Drug Enforcement Administration in the *New York Times*.

Not only does the daily supply of pot for America's street buyers—at an estimated $240 to $400 per pound—come via plane, but now the demand is so vast that ship smugglers are carrying the profitable cargo from Latin America to the New York area. Small, flagless freighters brought out of mothballs, or those about ready for the scrap yard, have been put into service for an organized-crime group, according to federal law-enforcement officials.

This shipping is now a multimillion-dollar operation, and officials believe it's the first time a major organized-crime faction has decided to get into the extensive marijuana trafficking.

"They are getting bolder and bolder," stated one government official.

Mr. Ralph Salerno, a former New York City police lieutenant and an expert on organized-crime affairs, who has been a consultant to congressional committees on organized crime, was quoted in a *New York Times* article, stating: "There's big money in marijuana now and even the image of selling pot isn't bad for the mob. You're not hooking ghetto kids on heroin. Instead, you're providing a commodity for college students and the middle class."

Nevertheless, United States authorities have seized some 5.1 million pounds of marijuana. The government is also training agents to use the air force's new AWAC (Airborne Warning and Control system), and this is expected to increase their capabilities of intercepting small aircraft. "Current attempts to stamp out Colombia's drugs still seem to be stopgaps, however, ineffectual against the tide of

Americans' demand for and tolerance of marijuana and co-caine," says Bensinger (USDEA chief). "Our efforts are so uphill that it is more than a challenge. The public attitude must change about drugs so the profitability for traffickers will decrease."

While the public turns away from the smokers, tokers, small- and big-time distributors, another industry has sprung up, called the "paraphernalia industry." One quarter of a billion dollars a year is spent on such things as Smoke Scope (a pipe for smoking pot), Supergrass (a process for growing marijuana), High Roller (for rolling cigarettes), Cannabis Indica (paper made from a blend of plants on Turkish, Pakistani, and Indian plantations).

The pot culture can locate paraphernalia in magazines such as *Hilife* and *High Times*. The latter claims to have 4 million readers. Another magazine, *Stone Age*, boldly advertises itself as "the all-new all-dope magazine. . . . The lavish new magazine by dopers for dopers. It's about your favorite leisure activities—pot, hash, coke, LSD and psilocybin and a host of other natural highs."

Such periodicals also carry market quotations of marijuana from Afghanistan to Hawaii. Qualities are listed—from "good" to "knockout"—with a list of prices on each.

It is obvious from all of this that marijuana is much more widespread than anyone can imagine. A multimillion-dollar industry has sprung up under our noses. It is so far out of hand, with so many people, countries, and products involved, that it would be virtually impossible to stop it without creating a new prohibition. Edward M. Brecher stated, in a Consumers' Union report on American drug policies in 1972, entitled *Licit and Illicit Drugs:* "It is now much too late to debate the issue: marijuana versus no marijuana. Marijuana is here to stay. No conceivable law-enforcement policy can curb its availability."

The Colombian Connection is well oiled. The routes are working like clockwork. The government controlling agencies do not have the money or manpower to do anything more than make periodic seizures. For each ship stopped or aircraft grounded, there are ten or twenty to take its place. And in spite of big headlines about key pushers being arrested in large cities, the traffickers will continue to smuggle into the country, and our youth will continue to "go up in smoke."

I favor strong law-and-order measures to try to prevent marijuana from reaching our nation's youth, but I realize that, at best, the government agency's work is more symbolic than substantive. Regardless, the symbolism is important.

Why? Because even if the flow of marijuana cannot entirely be stopped from reaching our kids, the continued efforts to confiscate it let everyone know that it is still a crime to transport and sell it. I happen to believe we can greatly reduce the amount of marijuana and other drugs coming into this country by having the will to declare war on the traffickers. But since I don't hold out much hope for that happening under present conditions, seizures are still important. They keep sending the message to the American public and to our youth that we do not believe marijuana should be legalized, that it is a dangerous drug, and that it still can get you sent to jail if you try to market it.

Not only are high-level efforts to arrest the pushers necessary; so is grass-roots detection. Some schools are conducting "strip searches," requiring students to strip naked while officials search for narcotics in their clothes.

A page-four headline in an upstate New York newspaper read: DOGS SNIFF OUT "POT" IN WEST POINT PARKING LOTS. The story stated that the dogs picked out two ounces of marijuana leaves, cigarettes, and residue in eleven cars owned by seniors in the United States Military Academy. While no arrests resulted, the academy was doing it to warn the cadets that the use of marijuana can mean dismissal.

Such actions are often controversial, and no vote or survey has yet been taken to find out how much of a school district condones such activity. One school principal claimed: "We receive a number of positive comments from people pleased that the school system is trying to protect students."

It is the above courageous actions (courageous in the sense that, given the liberalism in many schools, it takes a courageous and determined school administration to take a firm stand against marijuana use) which are necessary to keep the Colombian Connection from connecting with our youth. Perhaps—if books, pamphlets, and other material can once again be circulated in schools on the potential dangers of marijuana—the pot invasion from south of the border can at least be slowed down. If teachers, counselors, school-board members, clergymen, and parents learn the whole story on what pot is doing to our kids, more seizures, searches, sniffing, and the arrest of smugglers will take place.

If we don't do something, the marijuana epidemic is

certain to spread, and future generations will suffer the consequences in physical, psychological, emotional, and spiritual deterioration. Already kids are learning there is a price to pay, which they never bargained for when they took up the habit of "toking."

4

Grass Roots

An estimated 4 million high-school kids "cop a buzz" (a term chronic abusers use to describe the high they get from a joint) weekly. In all, of the 42 million Americans who are estimated to have experimented with marijuana, 8 to 10 million are probably regular to occasional users. But the figure may be as high as 16 to 20 million.

Who are these "grass roots" users?

Why do they smoke?

What do they think about marijuana?

How does it affect them?

How often and how much do the potheads smoke?

The high increase of teenage and preteen pot smoking is a direct result of the decriminalization laws. The increase is even greater on college campuses. Before decriminalization, I asked a university student why he did not smoke pot. He said, "Not because I don't want to. But the risk is too great. I don't want to blow a four-year education and a future career on a few joints."

Today the same type of student apparently feels safe enough to take the lesser risk of smoking marijuana in this age of decriminalization. A survey made by the army revealed that some 209,000 enlisted personnel in the United

States Army use marijuana and 49,000 use hard drugs, such as heroin and LSD.

In another survey, reported in the magazine *Your Place*, 1,721 respondents filled out a questionnaire telling when and why they go to pot. In an article entitled "Grass Roots Survey," 94 percent of the respondents had smoked marijuana at one time or another. The survey confirmed other studies, which show that the younger one begins smoking, the more likely he is to smoke regularly in later life. "For example, while 29.5 percent of those who started smoking at 14 or younger now smoke daily, that is so for only 9.4 percent of the individuals who started between the ages of 18 and 25, and 13.6 percent of those who started after 25."

What is most alarming is that a fourth of all current marijuana users are under 17. There is evidence that a proportion of them (about 4 percent) are 12 or 13 years old. Many youthful users are becoming more than occasional experimenters. Chronic use is on the upswing, turning many into potheads. In one survey, an estimated 11 percent of high-school seniors smoked pot regularly. That figure is up from 6 percent in 1975—thus it has almost doubled in less than three years. And the survey was only talking about seniors.

What is further alarming about teenage pot abuse is that, while the use of other drugs has stabilized, marijuana use is on a sharp rise.

School officials confirm that even some eight- and nine-year-olds are dragging on the weed. A young teenager interviewed by news commentator Edwin Newman on the NBC news special *Reading, Writing and Reefers* confessed that he smoked "about one hundred joints a week." Or, on an average, a little over ten a day.

Asked how many in school were on pot, he stated, "Only about twenty percent don't."

Kenny, another sixteen-year-old from a white, affluent neighborhood, said about his pot smoking, "I smoke mostly after school, but sometimes a group of us get together during school hours and share a joint. Occasionally, I'll cop a buzz on the way to school. I average about fifty to sixty joints a week, except when I go to a party. Then me and my friends will go through a whole bag." When asked if marijuana caused him to miss school, he revealed, "I've missed about ten to twelve days this term already."

Kenny is not a member of a street gang. He is not poor. His parents are professional people, and he has the ability to get good grades. But his life is increasingly centered around pot. Tragically, Kenny is typical of a new generation of habitual marijuana smokers, and he is one reason why it is time to take another look at our drug laws and drug attitudes. We are growing a generation of potheads. These young people are becoming psychologically addicted to marijuana and getting burned out.

"Burned out" is a term applied to chronic users who, because of extensive marijuana smoking, are no longer feeling the same effects from it. They have built up a psychological tolerance to it in their system. It may take them longer to get high, and they, in fact, may not even experience the normal high they once did. In other words, they are psychologically addicted. Instead of "copping a buzz" after one joint, it may take two or three.

Under normal conditions, users state they experience "a nice feeling" or that they "feel relaxed."

"I like to listen to music," said one.

"I like to talk. Yeah—talk a lot," stated another smoker.

"My buzz lasts for about an hour."

But the feeling and the effect changes for the long-term user. "I noticed," said one pothead, "that I wouldn't be myself anymore and I couldn't remember. People would say things to me, but I could not remember what was said."

Another revealed, "I don't do anything when I'm stoned. I am less aware. I feel drowsy. If I'm stoned in school, I may fall asleep in class."

While I was in talking to a group of present and former drug abusers (some had been confirmed addicts), they gave me the following comments about their use and abuse of marijuana and how it affected them:

"It makes you laugh when you don't want to laugh."

"It made me tired, lazy. . . . didn't want to do anything!"

"Sometimes I would get into a depressed state."

"Forget things. . . . I would go to the store to get onions for my mother and bring back rice. . . . can't reason."

"Someone would be talking to me and I'd drift away. . . . I was becoming a 'space cadet' slowly but surely."

"I'd get the 'munchies'—want to eat and eat. I'd finish dinner, smoke pot, then go right to the refrigerator to eat more. This would give me a splitting headache. . . . Eating also destroys the marijuana's effects and 'brings you down.' I'd go broke eating, smoking, and drinking."

When I asked them if it were possible to get burned out, they all responded immediately in the affirmative. "I needed a bag within a month," one told me. "The high wore off, so I started to put 'dust' [angel dust] on my pot to try and boost it. What's going to happen if it's legalized is the kids will run to the pusher to get angel dust or something else, 'cause legal stuff will soon wear off."

What about the nonphysiological effects of marijuana? In listening to the above group of drug abusers' comments, they confirmed another aspect of marijuana's danger, which in the long run is often more devastating than the physical or psychological damage: that is, the adverse effect on the user's life-style. Drug abuse can turn a good kid into a bad one. It can turn a mixed-up kid into a disturbed kid. And it can turn a normal youth into a social dropout.

Someone once wrote: "If all a drug does is kill you, it isn't so bad. It's the quality of life it provides you that should be of most concern."

Dr. Bloomquist, in *Marijuana: The Second Trip*, quotes a Dr. Milman on this matter.

> "Drugs blunt the pain of psychological conflicts that arise during that age period [adolescence] and post-pone problem-solving. The result is that such a young person emerges as an immature, drug-dependent, poorly integrated adult." The risk of marijuana use is compounded in this type of youngster, she noted, because they tend to experiment in their search for relief from psychic discomforts.

A person on marijuana may, for example, view what is normally a minor problem or situation as a major one. Lenny, a sixteen-year-old former pot smoker, told me, "I would get paranoia. Walking down the street, I would be constantly looking around, thinking someone was going to run up to me and pop me off or rip me off."

Abuse of marijuana tends to alter one's goals—and emotional and social drive. This "amotivational syndrome," as it is called, causes long-term users to become preoccupied with pleasure. Dr. D. Harvey Powelson, in private psychiatric practice in Berkeley, California, stated in a pamphlet titled *Our Most Dangerous Drug* and reprinted from *Listen* magazine:

> There's no question that people who use marijuana over a significant period of time are clearly in a state of not being interested in anything but feeling good. There are physiological explanations for that.
>
> Marijuana contains a chemical which affects the pleasure center. You get the illusion of feeling good. Then this illusion becomes more important than really feeling good. At the same time the effect of the drug is wearing off as you become tolerant of it. So you use more of it. And as that goes on, you either have to use stronger drugs or get another high. But this time the high is going to be a chemical or other false illusion, because you have lost the capacity to feel good in natural ways.
>
> At that stage, in the amotivational syndrome, people lose interest in everything else but the drug. And there are literally thousands of people who are only interested in getting high. They may have shifted from marijuana to heroin. A lot of them are shifting to alcohol, and this whole false question about mar-

ijuana and alcohol is going down the drain because we're seeing younger and younger alcoholics. First they begin combining the two, then they find out they can get drunker with alcohol than they can with marijuana.

Dr. Bloomquist quotes a letter from a mother, sent to the Los Angeles *Times,* but addressed to a candidate for district attorney who hoped to obtain votes by advocating the legalization of pot. She wrote:

> As a mother of an eighteen-year-old boy charged with possession of marijuana, I most emphatically say that I do not need scientific proof to see what damage it can do. I watched my son travel the typical road to ruin . . . from a student who enjoyed music, drama, and sports to a useless, filthy, college dropout with no aim in life other than to live in a carefree dream of distortion.
>
> He went all the way. Loss of appetite, long deep sleeps after the drug wore off, short attention span, poor memory, inability to read, talk, or even communicate for more than a few minutes. His continued defiance is a definite hindrance to his return to normal, as he has come to enjoy it so much.

A 1971 HEW report prepared for Congress tends to agree with this mother. It stated:

> The fact that there are many worldwide reports of heavy, chronic cannabis use resulting in a loss of conventional motivation and in social indifference is of particular interest in that there are now some reports

of somewhat similar findings among American heavy
users of marijuana.

It is impossible to know the total effect marijuana is
having on stunting the emotional and psychological growth
of youthful abusers. Yet, in some cases that I have witnessed
in the course of nearly twenty years' work in the drug-abuse
field, there has been enough indication of what might be
the total problem. And it is truly a sad loss of human potential. When I see promising, bright, likeable youth
turned into social dropouts who get sidetracked on the road
of life by what started as a few pleasurable puffs on a marijuana joint, I know what the experts mean when they talk
about the amotivational syndrome. No scientific research
can calculate such human and spiritual waste. But a multitude of brokenhearted parents know what this means.

Susan Bromwell, in an article published in *Good House-
keeping*, entitled "How I Got My Daughter to Stop Smoking Pot," quoted her daughter's thoughts about her marijuana use: "Pot weakens you. You lose your sense of self.
One drugged-out person is like another drugged-out person. . . . You may think you're getting yourself together
with pot, but you're not. You're pulling yourself apart."

The saddest conversations I have ever held have been
with parents describing the pain of watching their children
turn to a life-style that is totally alien to what both the
children and the parents ever knew before—or ever believed would happen—as a result of drug abuse.

"It's like a nightmare, Reverend," one father told me.
"Let alone what it is doing to my son—look what it's doing

to me. I holler and scream at my son. I'm not the same man I used to be. It's killed something inside me. I'll never be the same again. . . . to think that it all started when our son started hanging out down the street with a group of kids that were smoking pot."

Why do they smoke?

The young lady quoted above said, "It makes me forget my problems and tension. I'm relaxed, and nothing bothers me."

Older users have their own special reasons for turning to pot. "I don't get a hangover," stated one young adult woman. The *Your Place* survey found that only 3.1 percent of all respondents thought grass less benign than alcohol. Some 17.4 percent rated it a toss-up, and a whopping 79.1 percent considered grass less hazardous to the user's health (than alcohol). Some even considered it less harmful than tobacco—62.6 percent.

Sex is yet another reason why young adults use pot. The above-mentioned survey found that 43 percent cited the reason they valued marijuana most was to heighten their sexual experience.

Authorities are increasingly beginning to suspect there is a correlation between drug use and crime. We do know there is a connection between the use of alcohol and the committing of crime. Of the reported crimes, 50 percent are alcohol related. There are no studies available yet to show how much relationship there is between pot smoking and crime, *but*, if marijuana use follows a similar pattern to alcohol, then marijuana can directly or indirectly be a cause for criminal activities.

Dr. Bloomquist writes, in *Marijuana: The Second Trip:*

Attorney-General Haislip, from a paper presented
to the First National Conference on Student Drug
Involvement, University of Maryland, August 16,
1967, has argued that cannabis may stimulate criminal
activity in several ways: 1. It may be used by certain
criminals to fortify their courage prior to committing
crimes. 2. Chronic use of cannabis (usually hashish)
may produce general mental derangement and de-
moralization leading to criminal activity. 3. Pot use
may cause marginally adjusted persons to lower their
inhibitions and behave in an aggressive, antisocial
manner; and 4. Cannabis may cause panic, confusion,
or anger in otherwise normal persons who react adversely and then behave criminally as a consequence
of their mental disorder.

Yet there is a grass-roots movement of young adults bent
on perpetuating the idea that the marijuana smokers are
truly the "high class" of our society. I am alarmed when
I read, for example, in the drug-culture magazine *Hilife*,
the following editorial:

The fact of American society is changing. The generation that came of age during the 60's has produced
a new culture, a pot culture that cuts across all class
lines and, as a result, has had a great impact on the
traditional leisure class in America. . . . I call this
group the new high class, because leisure drugs have
played such an important part in bringing together
so many diverse segments of the population.

We, the new high class, are held together by more

than an interest in good dope. We have a sense of adventure. We're curious about the future and the newest trends. We believe in the equality of woman. We like dope, sex, having a good time—and want our pleasures now. Today, in 1979, we are the leisure class, an influential minority in America. *Tomorrow, we will be the democratic majority.* . . .

The new high class will be supporting efforts to abolish equally outdated federal and international laws that inhibit or prohibit the use of leisure drugs. In fact, sooner than most of us expect, leisure drugs will be designed by ethical pharmaceutical companies to increase our enjoyment of art, education, sports, sex and other useful and entertaining pursuits.

I shudder to think what future generations may have to face, if today's marijuana crusaders get their way. If marijuana is legalized—what next?

Underground scientists are now working on innovative drugs that may have the capability of drastically altering or manipulating the senses in ways never yet experienced. Researchers have already developed several pills that amplify specific senses. The dopers' magazine *Hilife* (February 1979), in an article entitled "Pleasure Drugs in the Year 2000," stated: ". . . pills can perform such precise functions as enhancing visual color sense or sensitizing auditory power, without intoxicating or inducing hallucinations in the user."

Other drugs that someday could be peddled at the local drugstore are:

Mescaline—which eliminates fatigue and boosts motivation.

Doet—which can focus the brain on specific thought patterns, which in effect can focus attention on previously unnoticed apsects of a situation.

Coco chewing gum—to provide a quick stimulant that lasts for a short span of time. It would have the same effect as a pill but last only thirty minutes or so.

We can also look for production of a more potent grass, such as hashish. What is not said behind the debate to decriminalize or legalize marijuana is the fact that many smokers will not be satisfied with low-grade, government-approved grass. This is evident by the increased amount of "good grass"—hashish and other stronger varieties of *Cannabis*—the police are confiscating. It is this higher grade stuff that has the potential of causing much more severe physical degradation and psychiatric disorders. As far back as 1968, the University of California, when asked to list the cases of adverse drug reactions they had treated in the past eighteen months, reported that the doctors in Los Angeles County said they had treated 2,389 patients who had taken LSD. In second place was marijuana, with 1,887 cases.

Experts believe that adequately high doses of the active principals of marijuana can induce a psychotic reaction in almost anyone.

It is evident from all of this that marijuana is not the innocent, mild, recreational drug that its proponents would like to lead us to believe. When all the above data, comments, and interviews with pot smokers are taken into consideration, they reveal that the users know only one side of the story of marijuana's effect. As we will see in the next chapter, many young people are truly confused about the scientific surveys on its harmfulness. Many kids get their information about marijuana only from their pot-smoking friends or from such magazines as *High Times*, which states, "Reefers are good for everybody, regardless of age." Yet the magazine contains no information whatsoever on its hazards.

That marijuana is a "mild, pleasurable drug no worse than alcohol" is a bill of goods being perpetrated on not only our American youth, but even on a nonsmoking adult population. Marijuana's harmlessness is a hoax and a falsehood. It is a trap that has a potential of harming perhaps millions of youth. *Changing Times* (March 1979) writes: "This trend towards use by children has caused second thoughts among some experts who in the past had not been unalterably opposed to the occasional recreational use of the drug by adults."

I do not want to overstate its possible damage to the bodies, minds, and characters of its users—but someone must set the record straight. It is true that previous generations used too many scare tactics to get kids off dope— especially marijuana. But this generation of users is just as guilty, in my estimation, with its casual "there's nothing to be concerned about" attitude. There is, right now, enough scientific and medical evidence piled up to blow the lid off all present arguments that have given rise to the decriminalization movement.

5

The Medical Case Against Marijuana

NORML (National Organization for the Reform of Marijuana Laws) made much to-do of a 1972 National Commission on Marijuana and Drug Abuse report (called the Shafer Commission). Its findings, prepared for the president and Congress and called *Marijuana: A Signal of Misunderstanding,* unanimously recommended "that possession of a small quantity of marijuana for personal use should not be a crime."

NORML, in a policy statement commenting on the Shafer Commission report, stated: "There have been no study results that have fundamentally changed the findings on which the Commission's recommendation was based."

NIDA Director Robert L. DuPont concludes, ". . . there is no question that alcohol and tobacco are causing us more health problems than marijuana does." (From *Marijuana— The Facts,* distributed by NORML.)

The commission further stated:

> From what is now known about the effects of marijuana, its use at the present level does not constitute a major threat to public health.
>
> Although a number of studies have been per-

formed, at present no reliable evidence exists indicating that marijuana causes genetic defects in man.

Until recently, the above statements went virtually unchallenged and were accepted as true statements by many government officials. *Now that all is changing*. No reasonable person today accepts the validity of the Shafer Commission report. Scientific and medical evidence now available reveals that our verdict pronouncing marijuana innocent and harmless, was, to say the least, premature. The American public has in effect been duped.

A growing number of past proponents of marijuana have now changed their minds as a result of the findings in the latest research on the drug. One such person is psychiatrist Dr. D. Harvey Powelson. He was quoted in 1967 as saying, "Marijuana is harmless. There is no evidence that it does anything except make people feel good. It has never made anyone into a criminal or narcotic addict. It should be legalized." He no longer holds to this theory.

Listen magazine asked him, "Why did you change your mind?"

His answer:

> Well, I was at the University of California when I made that statement. As director of the student health service, I was seeing a lot of patients and supervising people who were seeing many more. In the course of the next two years, either directly or indirectly, I saw literally thousands of students.
>
> One patient, whom I knew quite well and worked with for a long time, took up marijuana and hashish, which is a more concentrated form of marijuana, dur-

ing the time I was seeing him. It became clear to me and my wife, who also saw him, that there was something changing about his ability to think, to remember, to judge, to understand.

The things happening to his brain were things we could expect from someone who was having brain damage from alcohol or a tumor or organic brain damage. But he was a young healthy man. Then we discovered that the sessions that were particularly bad had occurred when he said he had used hashish within the previous two or three days. We both began to notice this connection.

Then I began to see the same connection in other patients. Since then, a lot of recent scientific evidence has supported and explained these observations.

I think marijuana is the most dangerous drug we have to contend with. . . .

Much of the argument, pro and con, over marijuana the past ten years has been based on erroneous information gleaned from inconclusive and often contradictory reports. Parents who oppose their children using marijuana have had too few facts based on irrefutable research at their disposal. The latest research, however, shows that marijuana is definitely a harmful and dangerous drug. For example, in a period between 1975–78, marijuana abusers were the second largest class of patients admitted for treatment at drug-abuse centers.

The proponents of legalized marijuana over and over again use the argument that "pot is harmless." Where do they get their data? Mainly from a few studies that produce seemingly inconclusive results. The key words here are "seemingly" and "inconclusive."

For example, one of the studies that the pro-pot lobby points to is the La Guardia Report. Mayor La Guardia, of New York City, set up a committee in 1939—made up of twenty-eight doctors, pharmacologists, psychiatrists, and sociologists—to investigate the effects of marijuana in the United States. The outcome was a study that stated, among other things, that: "Marijuana does not change the basic personality structure of the individual. It lessens inhibitions, and this brings out what is latent in his thoughts and emotions, but it does not make responses which would otherwise be totally alien to him." It also stated that no mental or physical deterioration resulted from prolonged use.

The La Guardia Report has had widespread publicity. Is it accurate? Does it, as the proponents of marijuana argue, justify a change in the laws to make marijuana available to any and all who desire it?

There are several problems in basing a more liberal attitude toward marijuana on the La Guardia Report or other similar past studies, such as the Shafer Commission quoted above. Such studies are inconclusive for several reasons:

1. **The strength of marijuana has changed.** As already reported in the previous chapter, Colombian hemp is ten times as strong as the marijuana that was in use on the streets four years ago.

2. **The age of present users is much younger.** Past studies centered on long-term users, such as musicians, artists, poets, and other artists, who use marijuana under

a more controlled life-style. Today, while the substance in the marijuana cigarettes is more potent, the age of the user is much younger. The combination of these two factors is producing much different results and effects on the user.

3. **Today's pot smoker is living in a different society.** Also, today's smoker is often using marijuana for different and additional reasons than previously used. The effects of marijuana have a lot to do with the social environment and physical constitution of the user at the time or place of smoking.

4. **Marijuana users are "smoking more and enjoying it less."** Past studies surveyed users who were occasional, part-time, and recreational users. Today's smokers are using pot in the same manner as the drinker uses alcohol. It is inevitable, then, that the physical and psychological effects on the user are going to be different than in the past.

What present-day studies reveal is that *pot is not harmless*. Most physicians involved in treating addicted patients agree that marijuana is a dangerous drug. New medical evidence is coming to the surface. The evidence is shocking and refutes the findings of past studies.

Hardin and Helen Jones, writing in their book *Sensual Drugs*, stated:

> Marijuana is the most controversial of the sensual drugs. Because short-term use seemed to have little adverse effect and because, until quite recently, little was known about how the drug affected body chemistry, it was assumed that marijuana was like other well-tolerated drugs and medication. It seemed less

harmful than other sensual drugs, and incidents of lethal overdose were rare. The fact that it was referred to as a "mild" hallucinogen reinforced the idea that it was harmless.

The truth is that in the 1960's, when marijuana first became popular, the public was unaware of the consequences of its use. The fad was new, and users had not yet experienced the long-term effects. "Authorities" appeared on every side, each contradicting the others. Alarmists exaggerated the negative evidence; optimists preached the safety and benefits of marijuana use. The fact that users could not see the harm that marijuana smoking was doing them complicated the issue. The facts, however, now rest on a firm scientific base; we now know some of the chemistry of the cannabis drugs and something of how they affect the body organs and cell functions.

The fact is no scientific evidence has been found to prove that marijuana is safe; we have only the personal testimonies of short-term users. [Author's emphasis.]

It is time, therefore, to set the medical and scientific record straight. Every parent, teenager (whether smoker or nonsmoker) teacher, clergyman, mental-health person—and others responsible for shaping the attitudes and opinions of the younger generation—must get this information out. It is time to counterbalance the carefully orchestrated public-relations campaign by the highly financed and powerful pro-pot lobbyists and other proponents, who would lead millions of kids to believe marijuana will not harm them.

The following is now known about marijuana's effects on its users.

The Brain

One of the most tragic revelations from studying marijuana's effect on long-term users is what is called the "cumulative effect." That is, marijuana stays in the body for a long period of time. Dr. Powelson, in the previously quoted *Listen* interview, stated:

> It stays in the brain, and it keeps operating long after people are high. This time element is anywhere from six weeks to six months. Biochemically, using tracers has proven that only half of the marijuana leaves your body in a week.
>
> Marijuana is soluble in oil and fat, and totally insoluble in water. The ratio is 600 to 1, so that once it gets inside the cell, it can't get back into the bloodstream the way other drugs do. If you drink alcohol, it is soluble in water and also in the bloodstream. As fast as you drink it, it goes into the bloodstream and continues to circulate, and then it is burned and leaves the body.
>
> Marijuana just stays there. When marijuana users get high—it usually takes them two or three times, because they have to build up a certain amount in their brain. Once they get high, they take another joint and get a little higher, then the high drops off and they think they are sober again. But the marijuana is still active. When three days later they take another joint then they get high again. But they are suffering the effects of marijuana all that time.

It could be called a cumulative effect, but what I am really talking about is the fact that marijuana stays active in the brain long after the user feels high. It is very deceptive. Since it doesn't lead to staggering or leave a smell on your breath, nobody else can tell that you are high and you don't know that you are high or whether you are stoned. Your brain isn't functioning right. And this can be proved. You can give a person mental tests before he takes a joint and then you can show that he can't do the same test as well for as long as 72 hours after the equivalent of 1 to 3 joints. It depends on the concentration.

If you ask somebody to take 100 minus 7 back to zero, he has to do two things at once. He has to remember what he is doing, and he has to keep track of the last number. It is not very complicated, but it is the kind of memory function that marijuana interferes with. Marijuana users tell that it focuses their attention. What that means is that they can't do two things at once. This particular memory test makes men do two things at once. If you time them on that test, it takes about 1½ minutes. Then they smoke three joints. A day later it will still take them 1½ minutes to do the same test.

In real life it is much more complicated. One of my patients was an airplane mechanic who worked on airplanes going from Alaska to Japan. He was staying stoned all the time. His supervisor didn't know it; nobody on the job knew it. He didn't care whether the instruments checked out or not. All he was interested in was staying stoned on the job. He wasn't thinking about anything but how good he felt. Yet pilots and passengers were depending on that man.

Right now some pilots in the mid-West are trying to get the Federal Aviation Agency interested in the fact that there are pilots and navigators and instrument testers who are stoned. Many people in this country—literally millions—are using marijuana and are stoned. And there may be people you and I are depending on to fly an airplane or drive a bus or perform our surgery, or drive on the highway.

Some interesting experiments have been undertaken by Dr. Robert G. Heath, professor and chairman, Department of Psychiatry and Neurology, Tulane University of Medicine, New Orleans, Louisiana, in which extensive studies were done on the brains of monkeys exposed to marijuana. The studies found that the animals, after smoking marijuana heavily, showed lasting changes in brain function. The changes were reflected in recordings from electrodes implanted into deep structures in the brain. Furthermore, the recorded changes continued to persist up until four months after they had stopped smoking. When Dr. Heath was asked, in an interview published by *Listen* magazine, if he could draw any conclusions and give any advice based on the hard facts of his study, he stated:

> Oh, yes. I think any agent that would affect a monkey would also affect a human. In view of this objective, scientific data, I would say that one would be unwise to expose himself to marijuana. It looks like a very damaging agent.
>
> We have seen these things go on in cycles. College

kids used to take amphetamines to stay awake to study. This went on for a couple of decades, until people began to realize how devastating "speed" was in terms of producing irreversible damage and creating behavioral problems. We are going to see the same thing happening with marijuana.

It is estimated that marijuana contains upwards of 300 chemicals, 60 of which are found in no other plant. The principal psychoactive ingredient in marijuana is known as tetrahydrocannabinol, or delta-9 THC. Doctors and researchers tell us that a few exposures to THC will not adversely affect the user, but it is the long-term accumulation of THC in the body that may damage body cells. No one really knows how long marijuana stays in the body. As much as 10 percent can remain as long as a week. Some studies have shown that, after 48 hours, more than half of the chemical breakdown products of marijuana were still in the body. Dr. Hardin B. Jones believes that:

> A week after a person smokes marijuana, 30 percent is still in the body in the active form. There is no other drug or medication that I know of that lingers in the body so long. Of the portion that remains, the body retains 70 percent of that longer than the second week. It gets rid of only 10 percent a month or after, so the burden stays in the body for a long time, and as a person uses more and more, it accumulates.

It may be that the heavy pot smoker is never free of some of the effects of both THC and other ingredients in pot.

Reproductive Organs

Studies have shown that 44 percent of the THC females (laboratory-tested female monkeys) who had been given the human equivalent of one to three reefers a day, did not produce healthy, living offspring. The mothers lost their babies during pregnancy by abortion or stillbirth, or by infant death soon after birth. (In comparison, the control group of undrugged monkey mothers had a 12 percent birth loss.) Other studies, on human females who smoked pot one to three times daily for at least six months prior to the studies, found that 38.3 percent of the women who smoked pot had defective menstrual cycles, compared to 12.5 percent in a control group of nonsmokers. Dr. Hardin Jones believes that "genetic damage is a very real risk." In a September, 1977, *Listen* magazine article, he stated:

> Marijuana is a most threatening substance known. No other environmental hazard is as likely to influence the health of those yet to be born. Persons smoking marijuana should pause and reflect on their responsibility for the health of their future children.

One of the most startling findings to come out of the International Symposium on Marijuana held in Reims, France, July 22 and 23, 1978, was the report a scientist at the conference gave on marijuana's effect on the male sperm. Scientists stated that there was a below-normal sperm count in both animals and humans exposed to marijuana, as well as a marked increase in sperm abnormality. "Banana-shaped heads, formless heads, and broken hooks," were produced in the sperm by marijuana.

The message must be spread far and wide, to both the habitual and the occasional marijuana smoker: He may be playing genetic roulette.

Lungs

It is utterly foolish for anyone, be it the smokers or high-ranking government officials, to think that—in the words of the 1972 Shafer Commission report to Congress and the president—marijuana "use at the present level does not constitute a major threat to public health." This is especially true when there is so much medical evidence linking tobacco smoking with lung cancer and other diseases. Marijuana is classified as a drug—tobacco is not. To believe tobacco is dangerous to one's health and marijuana is not is to be either naive or ignorant.

Marijuana has more tar in a stick than does a cigarette. The cancer-producing elements in tobacco are carcinogens. Marijuana has more of these agents in it than tobacco, and it stays in the lungs longer and gets down deeper in the bronchial tubes. Studies have shown that those who smoke marijuana for an extended period may develop chronic bronchitis and emphysema. Tobacco smokers have to puff for ten to twenty years before lung diseases appear; among hashish smokers, it can take as little as six to fifteen months. This is because *one marijuana joint is the same as smoking one pack of cigarettes*. As a result, the user's lungs are blacker, due to the fact that the marijuana must be inhaled deeper and held in the lungs longer. *Sensual Drugs* states: "Autopsy examination of the lungs of heavy marijuana smokers shows extreme breakdown in lung structure."

Studies have also shown that extended marijuana use

produces a marked reduction in white-cell response, the body's prime defense against infection. THC seems to reduce the lungs' capacity to kill bacteria. Thus marijuana smokers are more susceptible to colds, flu, and other normal germ infections.

Hardin and Helen Jones, in their book *Sensual Drugs,* list eight principal dangers of marijuana use. They are as follows:

1. Unlike the other sensual drugs, marijuana's effects are usually not experienced the first few times a user takes it. Then, for a time, a very small dose produces an effect, which leads the user to believe that marijuana is indeed harmless.

2. Because of the mildness of early withdrawal symptoms (as compared with those from other sensual drugs), the user thinks he is taking a mild drug and can easily withdraw any time he chooses.

3. Psychological conditioning to marijuana, in comparison with the apparent lack of chemical dependence, is strong. The user is dependent on marijuana before he realizes it; a few regular or heavy users can stop without great effort.

4. The toxic substances in marijuana accumulate in the brain and the body tissues and will leave slowly. Most users do not know that most cumulative, noxious substances have long-range effects that are not evident from short-term use. Even mild use of marijuana (regular social use, for example) produces some long-lasting effects.

5. Tolerance to marijuana builds up so rapidly that most regular users need to progress to stronger or

larger doses, or to use the drug more frequently to feel the effects. What originally was a pleasant experience, in time is repeated only to avoid feeling bad. The majority of marijuana users do not stay with the occasional smoking of a mild marijuana cigarette.

6. The mechanisms in the brain that the user needs to evaluate his situation are disturbed by marijuana. The user, even when he is severely affected, cannot understand his problem.

7. For various reasons, many marijuana users tend to become smokers of tobacco, to use alcohol excessively, and to go on to use stronger drugs. The effect from a combination of drugs is compounded, not simply the sum of the effects of each.

8. Marijuana use has spread in epidemic proportions among the young, who have the most to lose from it. Marijuana can retard emotional development at a critical time in the maturing process. The adolescent is especially vulnerable, as he is developing new habits and ideas and integrating his personality into his surroundings. Sensual drugs alter body functions normally controlled by hormones. Now we know that hormone production is disturbed by marijuana. Sex hormones, delicately balanced in the adult, are in a state of flux in the adolescent.

The Joneses, in introducing the above material, stated: "We should look upon marijuana as the most potentially dangerous of the sensual drugs. We know now that its effects are deleterious, but insidious and subtle. Even so, the full extent of its harmfulness is probably yet to be learned."

When the latest findings are looked at objectively, there can be no other conclusion than that of the former director of NIDA (National Institution of Drug Abuse) Dr. Robert L. DuPont, who made the following statement in *Listen* magazine:

> I get a very sick feeling in the pit of my stomach when I hear talk about marijuana being safe. Marijuana is a very powerful agent which is affecting the body in very many ways. What the full range of these consequences is going to prove to be, one can only guess at this point. But from what we already know, I have no doubt that they are going to be horrendous.

This comment is especially significant since it was Dr. DuPont whom I quoted earlier in this chapter as saying, "There is no question that alcohol and tobacco are causing more health problems than marijuana does."

Dr. DuPont told NBC news commentator Edwin R. Newman that he had changed his mind about marijuana, in that he now felt badly that he had contributed to the idea that marijuana was not dangerous.

The time has come for Congress, the police, local authorities, our schools and churches, and parents to discover what Dr. DuPont has learned about the marijuana controversy and take a stand against its decriminalization and legalization.

Presently many in society have committed themselves to a position on marijuana that, in the light of the above evidence, must be reconsidered.

6

Decriminalization—Blessing or Curse?

A PAPERBACK NOVEL entitled *Acapulco Gold* stated on its inside cover the scenario for the future of legalized pot:

> To: MK & C
> From: THE CLIENT
> THE PRODUCT: MARIJUANA
> The next President of the United States will legalize marijuana. We want to sell it to the American people.
> THE MOTIVE: MILLIONS OF DOLLARS
> The race is on. We're ready to grow and ship it. Can you sell marijuana like cigarettes? And can you do it first?
>
> Read what happens in an advertising agency when it gets the jump on the promotion of the first legal marijuana cigarettes. And, read what happens to the creative director handling the account, torn between the exciting campaign that would make history and his fears that, reports to the contrary, he is actually selling a dangerous drug.

The above is not science fiction. The prospects of Madison Avenue being able to launch a campaign to get your children and teenagers to turn on to pot may be just around the corner. If so, can other drugs, even more potent and dangerous, such as cocaine, heroin, and other twenty-first-century drugs and highs be far behind?

The major crusade organization for decriminalization and eventual legalization is NORML (National Organization for the Reform of Marijuana Laws). Its small staff of full-time workers and a budget of over one-half million dollars a year "supports the removal of all criminal and civil penalties for the private possession of marijuana for personal use. The right of possession should include cultivation and transportation for personal use, and the casual nonprofit transfers of small amounts of marijuana."

The above quote, taken from a pamphlet entitled "Official NORML Policy 1977," is this pro-pot organization's stated policy and definition of the decriminalization of marijuana.

Decriminalization should not be confused with legalization. The latter would pave the way for commercialization of it, like liquor or tobacco. The goal of organizations like NORML, and others who advocate decriminalization, is, I believe, a first step to campaigning for its legalization. Once the more liberalized laws are in effect and the general public has gotten accustomed to the relaxed attitude, you can be sure the crusade to legalize will be pushed as hard as the present drive to decriminalize.

For now, the aim is to change the penalties for possession of small amounts of marijuana.

The marijuana laws did, and do yet, in some cases, need changing. Some past and present laws treat marijuana use on the same level as heroin and other hard drugs. This was and is unfortunate and a mistake that should be corrected.

Such severe laws have been used by the proponents of decriminalization as a justification for passing more lenient laws.

Changing Times reports:

> In Missouri a college student is serving a seven-year sentence after he was convicted of selling $5-worth of marijuana to an undercover agent, and a twenty-year-old woman, convicted of splitting an ounce of the stuff with a date who turned out to be an undercover agent, was recently paroled from a five-year term in a prison farm there. An appeal to the courts by the young man with the help of NORML was denied and a letter-writing campaign coordinated by the organization failed to change the Governor's mind about the sentence. Now the constitutionality of the law is being challenged.

Such cases do point out the imbalance in drug sentences. But the pendulum is swinging now toward the side of tolerance. The Missouri student and other similar cases are used by organizations like NORML to gain sympathy for their decriminalization cause.

Eleven states—Alaska, California, Colorado, Maine, Minnesota, Mississippi, Nebraska, New York, North Carolina, Ohio, and Oregon—have decriminalized marijuana. What this means is that possession of a small amount of marijuana, usually an ounce or less (enough for about fifty cigarettes), may result in a fine but no jail term, or (depending upon circumstances) no criminal record. In Oregon, possession of up to an ounce is a civil offense on the same level as a traffic violation, carrying a maximum fine of $100. In Maine, the fine is up to $200, in Mississippi, $250.

Anyone caught with more than the maximum allowable amount may face the felony charge of possession with intent to sell. But in approximately forty other states, pot smoking is still risky business and the smoker faces stiff fines, a jail term, and/or felony conviction. In Arizona, for example, a person convicted three times on a simple pot-possession charge can be imprisoned for life. However, generally courts are deemed more lenient in sentencing pot offenders, as they respond to the public's changing attitudes. Some judges are still handing down strong punishments, however.

What has been the effect of the reformed laws? Is decriminalization working?

One of the most outspoken foes of the new laws is former Los Angeles police chief Ed Davis. "Decriminalization has increased the amount of marijuana, stimulated the use and trafficking," says Davis.

"We had been reducing the use of marijuana through good law enforcement. In 1971, the Los Angeles police department seized 16,392 pounds of marijuana. By 1975, we only picked up 4,990 pounds—because we were discouraging its use. But in 1976, after decriminalization, we seized 17,916 pounds."

Davis did concede that the law charging marijuana smokers with a felony was too harsh. "Possession should be in the same class as intoxication, an arrestable misdemeanor," he stated.

A study prepared for the White House by a presidential

panel set up in 1973 and revised by Carter in 1977—called the Strategy Council on Drug Abuse—stated:

> The past use of incarceration as a sanction against marijuana use has been irrationally applied, often with an extremely harsh punishment doing more harm to the individual than the drug itself.

But the report recommends that "the penalty should not be lifted altogether as this could be misconstrued to mean we condone marijuana use."

There is no doubt that the new laws are increasing the use and abuse of marijuana. A *U.S. News and World Report* article stated, "Among high school seniors, the proportion who used marijuana daily almost doubled in three years, from 6 percent in 1975 to 11 percent last year. A 1977 survey showed that 56 percent of all seniors had tried marijuana or a related drug, hashish; 48 percent said they had tried it in the past year, and 26 percent admitted using it weekly."

I believe these figures are very conservative. Pot is the new alcohol of this generation. I can hardly attend a major sporting event in the New York area or go anywhere where large numbers of youth are gathered without sniffing the distinct aroma of marijuana.

The decriminalization of marijuana has in effect said to young people, "Pot is okay." However, the lawmakers are talking out of both sides of their mouths. On the one hand, they say it's okay to smoke it, but on the other hand, they say it's not okay to sell it. By giving the okay to smoke it, they have opened the floodgates for the smugglers, traffickers, and the pushers. If it's okay to smoke it, in essence, they are saying it must be all right to sell it as well.

Even in states that have not officially decriminalized marijuana, there seems to be an unofficial policy to be lenient on the smokers.

What have been and what will be the results of decriminalization on our society?

1. **Boys and girls will be smoking marijuana at younger ages.** Where states have lowered the drinking age, surveys show one result is that younger kids start drinking more. The twelve-, thirteen-, and fourteen-year-olds who hang out with the older kids start drinking with their friends. The same pattern seems evident among teen pot smokers.

What frightens me is the fact that the older, more stable youth may smoke pot for pure pleasure, but introduce some younger teen, who has personal or family problems, to the habit and he starts using marijuana as a crutch. In my experience, drug abuse can turn a minor emotional disturbance in a teenager's life into a severe emotional problem. Older youth usually are better able, and have matured enough, to face the realities of life. Young teens have not yet found alternate means of coping with problems, as adults often do. If smoking marijuana becomes the teenager's method of coping, he may never find a solution and become an habitual dropout or cop-out from society.

2. **Wherever marijuana is pushed, there are often other drugs available.** In the '60s, the argument against pot was that it always led to heroin. And that was true, years ago in the ghetto. But when millions of middle-class youth

started to smoke marijuana, the majority did not go on to hard stuff. The idea that marijuana led to hard-core addiction was abandoned; but it shouldn't have been, entirely. My experience shows that for some types of youth, marijuana does become a lead-in drug to other more powerful and dangerous drugs. For example, cocaine is now the drug of choice among the more socially elite, while angel dust is the companion drug to marijuana on the streets.

I am convinced that anyone who starts using marijuana regularly and is given the right (I should say wrong) set of circumstances, will experiment with other, more potent, drugs. This is the risk the pot smoker takes. The proponents of decriminalization have used this as an argument for controlling marijuana, or even legalizing it. They say, "Take marijuana out of the hands of the illegal pusher and put it in the hands of government-controlled distributors, as is done with alcohol and tobacco. Thus we'll avoid having our kids buying pot from the street-corner pusher."

Were marijuana to be legalized, it would of necessity have to have its potency strictly controlled. Legalized pot would thus be in a mild form. Regular users would not get the desired effect. To be sure, the pusher would be there with better stuff. Decriminalization or legalization will not eliminate the black market in marijuana. And it's the illegal trafficker who has access to other dangerous drugs. To be sure, decriminalization or legalization will not put him out of business.

3. **Look for decriminalization to increase the number of addicts in our society.** My brother David and I wrote, in our book *The Untapped Generation*, a list of ten reasons

how and why young people experiment with and become dependent upon drugs. It would be appropriate to list them at this point:

The curious.   Some young people are always curious about something that is mysterious, adventurous, dangerous, and illegal. But while curiosity is given as an excuse for having started a habit, it is often later found out that some character defect perpetuated the drug-taking.

The weak willed.   Some young people seek a simple, quick, magical solution to the problems of life and to their own character defects. Such young people need little urging to get them started and they find it difficult to put down the habit once it has been fixed. These include the severely inadequate, immature, and the lost and depressed.

The social addict, or the social give-ins.   These are young people who take drugs because it is the sociable thing to do. In their clique, everyone is doing it. Not to do so would mean to be left out. Taking drugs is a prerequisite for belonging to some groups.

The sense seekers.   These are made up of the more artistic types who are seeking breakthroughs or a renewal of their creative power. They perpetually seek to spring free of their ordinary way of seeing or sensing the world around them.

Some users claim to have understood themselves better after taking the mind-expansion drugs. One boy said, "My mind opened up—I found out a lot of things about myself I didn't know—but I didn't like what I found. And I have no ability to do anything about the things I learned."

The escapers. These are young people seeking escape from boredom, responsibility, frustration and anxiety. Many are affluent youths who have become bored with blessings. They don't know how to get high on life. They cannot accept responsibilities or the difficulties that make a young person grow. Life turns them *in*, not *on*.

The accidental drug user. This is a young person who has been turned on to drugs by a friend, relative, or some older person. The young person taking the drug did not really know what he was getting involved in, and accidentally got hooked.

One fellow related, "My best friend gave me a marijuana joint. Although I knew it was dangerous, I trusted him and so I thought everything would be all right. I had a pleasant drug experience and so started smoking from time to time with him until I woke up one day and found myself hooked." Although in the latter case, the young man was not completely naive to the drug scene, he nevertheless became accidentally involved because he trusted a friend.

The persuaded addict. Related to the social and the accidental user are those who have been persuaded to indulge. A husband persuades his wife; a boyfriend turns on his girl friend. The user may go along because of some misguided sense of love, or—in the case of some girls—because of some idea that if she were involved, she would be able to help her man with his drug problem.

The prescription addict. Some get involved in drug addiction through physical problems for which the doctor prescribed a certain drug. However, they find that while the drug alleviates their physical problem, it creates a worse one in that they develop a psychological dependence of which they are unaware. Prescription addicts are often people who started their drug use under extreme stress.

Stone heads. This is the type of young person who has found absolutely no meaning or value in life. He has come to the conclusion that anything is better than what he has experienced. He will take anything and everything, perhaps even a combination of drugs and alcohol.

The religious seekers. A growing number of young people use drugs as a religious sacrament. They seek personal insights or religious experiences. More frequently, they use psychedelic drugs (LSD and others). They are searching, and believe that these drugs open up new levels of spiritual understanding.

Marijuana has the potential to introduce the entire drug world to each of these ten types of indulgers. To many—perhaps millions—marijuana, and marijuana alone, is the drug of choice. They smoke pot but do not indulge in other more dangerous drugs. *But there are a percentage of marijuana smokers who turn from being regular users to regular abusers and then go on deeper and deeper into the drug scene, eventually getting themselves hooked, either physically or psychologically, or both.* The more pot smokers, the more potential for a percentage going on to the real addictive drugs. It is this percentage—as small as it may be in proportion to the total number of pot smokers, yet numbering in the tens and hundreds of thousands—that strict marijuana laws are intended to protect. If we can ban a dangerous food additive that could cause cancer to a very small percentage of Americans, then by the same reasoning we must provide strict laws to control a substance that has the potential of destroying even a small percentage of our total youth.

4. **Increased death and injury on the nation's highways.**   When the first talk about liberalized marijuana laws was advanced, I stated, "The potentially most dangerous result of widespread marijuana use is going to take place on the nation's highways. In addition—how would you like your doctor to be puffing on a joint before operating on you, or the pilot of your airplane, or the taxi or bus driver?" Until recently, there has been almost a total unawareness of drivers who are intoxicated on pot. Most states have tests to establish alcohol intoxication, but there is as yet no effective test to detect drivers who are under the influence of marijuana.

According to an article in the May, 1979, *Reader's Digest*:

> "A growing number of stoned motorists are endangering lives on the highways. . . . Recent studies blow the warning whistle on a little-publicized but nonetheless frightening new menace to motorists; the pot smoker driving "high" on the highways. Persuasive evidence is mounting that such drivers often have a distorted sense of space and time, altered peripheral

and central vision, impaired manipulative and coordinative skills.

Relaxed pot laws have given smokers the idea they can smoke their weed anytime and anyplace they want, similar to lighting up a cigarette. This is putting potentially dangerous maniacs behind the wheel of an automobile, adding to the already outrageous problem of the drunk driver. Richard L. Burton, former commissioner of Alaska's Department of Public Safety, quoted in the above-mentioned *Reader's Digest* article, stated: "The alcohol problem on the highways will soon be only half as serious as marijuana— and that's not because alcohol is going to get any better."

In 1975, the Boston Traffic Accident Research Team surveyed 267 drivers declared "most responsible" for a fatal accident and found 16 percent had been smoking marijuana prior to the accident.

A California Department of Justice study, in which 1792 blood samples were taken from drivers arrested for traffic accidents or for driving under the influence of drugs, found 16 percent had sufficient THC in their blood to constitute marijuana intoxication. Only one-half of the drivers arrested had agreed to give a blood sample.

Some tests have shown that drivers under the influence of a large dose of marijuana show a decline of 42 percent in driving skills, and the high-dose subjects had a 63 percent decline. Other studies show "a definite decrease in skills and performance five to six hours after taking a strong social dose of marijuana . . . and lingering effects as long as twenty-four hours later."

The worst part about the marijuana-intoxicated driver is his ability to conceal it and his unawareness of how his ability is impaired. The drunk driver usually finds it difficult to hide his condition, especially if stopped by the police. *Reader's Digest* states, "This apparent ability to 'hide the high' gives many pot smokers confidence that they can drive stoned."

Even NORML recognizes the danger of driving under the influence of marijuana and "strongly discourages the driving of automobiles or other vehicles while under the influence of marijuana or any other drug, and recognizes the legitimate public interest in prohibiting such conduct."

5. **Decriminalization of marijuana will result in economic loss to our nation.** We already have two serious intoxicants draining the nation's economy—tobacco and alcohol. Nicotine is said to cost us 60,000 to 300,000 deaths per year and over $20 billion in economic loss.

Alcohol has produced nearly 10 million alcoholics. The financial, social, and human waste this has brought upon society is so pervasive there is hardly any area of our lives not affected by it. An estimated 100,000 persons yearly die from alcohol's effects, with an economic loss of $30 billion.

Are we ready to add another intoxicant—marijuana—to these two? P. Zeidenberg, in a report to a United States Senate hearing in 1974, stated:

> . . . there is no question in my mind that legalization of marijuana will lead to a large population of chronic heavy marijuana users, numbering in the millions, just as prevails with alcohol and tobacco. Both of these latter agents exact a terrifying toll in human life, suffering and expense in this country annually. I think it is probable that heavy marijuana use in our country would create a third at-risk population,

overlapping only in part with the two previous groups, and further add to mortality, morbidity and public cost.

6. **International repercussions.** Some of our foreign allies do not understand why America is flirting with the legalization of marijuana. In countries like South Africa, Brazil, Turkey, and Greece, where *Cannabis* has been used for centuries, they now have severe laws banning its use.

Egypt had such an epidemic of marijuana use during Nasser's rule. He spent a lot of money for an extensive study of marijuana. It was undertaken by an American-trained scientist and published in ten volumes in Arabic. It showed, in a very scientific way, that without question, marijuana affects people's ability to function.

The United States is part of an international agreement with other nations to "limit exclusively to medical and scientific purposes, the production, manufacture, export, import, distribution of, trade in, use and possession of drugs."

Many people in our Justice Department feel that if our marijuana laws are relaxed too far, our positions on harder drugs will be in jeopardy in terms of our agreements with other countries.

It is interesting to note, as has one Swedish authority:

> Demand for legalizing cannabis has been strongest in those countries which have had the shortest experience and the weakest form of the drug. In all the twenty-one countries my wife and I visited during a study of drug-abuse problems, and particularly in the countries where cannabis use is endemic, people were

dismayed to hear of the attempts in the U.S. to legalize marijuana. They felt that legalization would allow drug use to spread through the entire population . . . and it is felt to be a factor in keeping the poor impoverished.

7. **The drive to decriminalize is a calculated step by the proponents of marijuana to legalize it.** At first the advocates of decriminalization claimed, in their testimony before state legislatures preparing to vote on decriminalization laws, that they did not favor legalization. Yet, within weeks after such state laws were passed, these same people began making speeches calling for full-scale legalization.

The decriminalization people use their campaign as a front and a smoke screen to hide their legalization movement, because they know the public is not ready for the latter—yet.

In New York State, the marijuana lobbyists got behind a bill to legalize marijuana for medical purposes (it is said to aid the sight of those suffering from glaucoma). Again the purpose was to "get whatever we can," as one marijuana advocate stated.

An organization calling itself Committee for the Abolition of Marijuana Prohibition (CAMP) claims to be pressing a nationwide voter-registration drive prior to the 1980 presidential election under the banner LEGALIZE MARIJUANA— REGISTER TO VOTE. A spokesman for the group stated: "We have to make politicians aware that those people who are out in the streets demonstrating are registering to vote," and they feel Carter owes them a debt, in that many voted for him in 1976 because they thought he would push for the legalization of pot after the last election.

If I can find any benefit in the results of decriminalization of marijuana, it has been the opportunity to weigh the full impact legalization would have on our nation's youth and the whole of society. The prospect of machine-packaged legal pot being sold over the counter is one of the most frightening prospects that faces this and future generations. It could have a devastating impact on our teenage and young-adult life-styles. I hope we've seen enough already to make us want to call a halt to the move to further decriminalize or legalize marijuana.

7

How to Guard Kids Against Drugs

DRUG PREVENTION must begin in the cradle.

I wrote, in my book entitled *Fast Track to Nowhere* (which deals with the shocking facts about teenage drinking):

> Drug and alcohol prevention is not so much a classroom program of education as it is a process of continual education in the home. . . . The two greatest factors in causing teenage drinking [the same can be said for marijuana] are peer pressure and parental influence. The best of homes and parents can do little to remove the child or teen from the pressures to drink they will face in school, at extracurricula activities or among neighborhood youth. But children who have their physical, emotional, and spiritual needs met at home, have the best chance of not caving in or giving in to peer pressure when it comes to drinking, using drugs, sexual promiscuity, and other teenage "curiosities."

I believe there are a few important things parents can do to create a right atmosphere in the home and instill in their children the necessary character to help them face the inevitable outside influences (be it pot or whatever).

I would like to list here the home remedies for drug prevention as adapted from chapter 8 of *Fast Track to Nowhere*, entitled "Prevention."

1. **Properly communicate a value system when talking or teaching on the dangers or evils of drugs.** This is the generation that asks "Why?" In answer to a question as to why they are using drugs, the answer "Why not?" may come back. They feel "It's my body" and thus they have a right to get high. When parents flatly state "no drugs," they are going to have to give valid reasons why not and communicate them through not only words but by the example of their own life-styles. Studies have been conducted that show kids whose parents abuse alcohol, pills, and other medications are more likely to use marijuana and other drugs themselves.

Parents must create a good communication atmosphere with their kids to discuss marijuana on a factual level, not purely on an emotional level, such as, "I'd better not catch you smoking pot!" Parents must give their kids valid reasons why not when it comes to drug experimentation and drug abuse.

Dr. Edward Bloomquist states:

> One of the biggest problems where marijuana is concerned is that adults and youth have remarkably different values. If the adult insists that marijuana is *all* bad and the youngster assumes that marijuana is *all* good, neither group can develop a common ground upon which to discuss the problem. Each must un-

derstand from the beginning what the drug means to the other person to be able to discuss it in this context. They can learn from each other.

A young person needs a reason not to smoke pot, other than to be told, "Because I said so." I hope the parent or counselor will have found some of those reasons in this book.

2. **Learn to "defuse" rebellion.** Marijuana was the protest drug of the '60s. It is no longer used by the masses of youth as an outward symbol of rebellion, but it may be, on an individual basis. One youth told me, "I knew it would send my old man up a wall if he heard I was smoking pot. I wanted him to know—to hurt him."

His was a case of a broken father-son relationship. However, the lad was not only rebelling but crying out for attention. He wanted to be caught. More importantly, he wanted to be caught in his father's arms, or at least gain some attention. It is sad but true that some kids can only be noticed by parents if they do something wrong or drastic to get attention.

I firmly believe parents can defuse rebellion, as I said in *Fast Track to Nowhere*:

> The time to watch is when children are between twelve and fourteen. Some do reach stages of rebellion sooner or even later, depending on circumstances at home and school. But generally speaking, the critical stage and ages are twelve to fourteen. This is when the adolescent is trying to find himself and flex the emotional muscles of his very own individual per-

sonality. It is a period when he is full of contradictions, finding that he is torn between being the child of adolescence and becoming the emerging young adult.

Parents must remember that outside the home, kids are made to feel that to be "in," or to be accepted, they must drink or smoke a joint. Kids are torn between these two internal and external worlds at a time when it is normal for them to challenge their parents' standards and values and to see how far they can stretch the limits of parental authority. They are also trying to make up their minds as to their own personal convictions.

Bloomquist says:

> There comes a time in a youngster's life when it is very important for him to isolate himself at times from his family to establish his own identity. Family activities up to the age of fourteen or fifteen are critical. At this point, however, parents should recognize that youngsters have a definite need to build their own particular world.

> Unfortunately, we are not always willing to let youth experiment. Yet when they become involved in activities which are abhorrent to parents, some adults may try to interrupt their "flight from the nest." This is an error because the child, if he is healthy, will find a way to escape even if it means alienating himself from his parents. Critically, youth needs support, emotional and frequently financial, from their parents up to and through their mid-twenties now that the educational jungle has extended its boundaries. Most cannot be cut off prematurely without

serious psychological disruption, but neither will they permit adults to smother them if they have any aggressive spark of life.

In *Fast Track to Nowhere*, this is related to Christian youth:

> Christian youth, especially, go through periods of rebellion against the church and the things of God. They begin questioning the spiritual values and precepts they have been raised on. Such rebellion is natural and can produce positive results. Teens come to the age of "accountability" when they must choose for themselves as to whether they are going to follow Christ or Satan. Many choose to go their own way and only after years of wandering, does the prodigal come home.
>
> Such rebellion does not need to lead to backsliding or kids getting "turned off" to the church and spiritual things. Parents can help by preparing for and accepting the fact of such rebellion. When the child is younger, the limits must be narrow. But the older the adolescent is, the wider must be the limit of his questioning and of permissible behavior. Ultimately, our youth have to make up their own minds about drugs, alcohol, sex, God, church, et cetera. As they mature, the limits need to be broadened until they are ready to make their own personal decisions.

3. **Listen for the "feel."** Words are windows to the soul. As I said in *Fast Track to Nowhere*, "Expressed rebellion can be a sign or signal to the parent of a deeper problem. Therefore, what the teenager is saying may not

necessarily be what he means or 'feels.' *Listen for the feel.*"

In the above-mentioned incident of a young man who said he wanted to hurt his father, he was in truth only reflecting his own internal hurt. It is a wise and discerning parent who is sensitive enough to know that behind his child's words and actions are feelings that may be a sign his child is saying something different or directly opposite from what appears on the surface.

The art of listening involves listening on three levels: listening to what is said, listening to what has not been said (what was left out), and listening for what *cannot* be said because it lies buried deep in the emotions.

Parents who have the right kind of relationship with a child will, on most occasions, know intuitively when the child is hurting or feeling down. Major doses of love and understanding will keep such a youngster from trying to block or escape the hurt by taking drugs, and encourage him to open up and talk about it.

4. **Let your teenager (or any child) know he or she is someone special.** Ann Landers, in an article printed in *Reader's Digest* entitled "What You Do and Don't Owe Your Children," states:

> What do parents owe their children? One of the chief obligations parents have to give their children is a sense of personal worth. Self-esteem is a cornerstone for good mental health. A youngster who is continually criticized and "put down," made to feel stupid and inept, constantly compared with brothers, sister, or cousins who do better, will become so un-

sure, so terrified of failing, that he or she won't try at all.

The child who is repeatedly called "bad" or "noddy," or "no good" will behave in a way that justifies the parents' description. Children have an uncanny way of living up—or down—to what is expected of them.

It is unfortunate that many parents were raised during the "silent years," when their parents never verbalized approval, only discipline. It has been carried over in this generation into two extremes: parents who give their children everything but praise, or parents who give their children neither.

5. **Establish firm and consistent ground rules.**   Between parents and teens there are tensions—good ones—pulling at each other. One is the parents trying to enforce the limits they want their kids to operate within, and the kids stretching those or rewriting the line according to their own standards. In between the two lines, like tension wires, is what is popularly called "the generation gap." I believe such tensions are healthy. However, parents should stick to their standards, even though their kids are ultimately writing their own book of rules. Surprisingly, I find the troubled kids we work with want their parents to be strict (but fair). Even though they rebel and try (and do) at times break the rules, down deep inside they have a feeling that parents who bug them (in the right way) do care for them. Kids who grow up in families where the morals and standards are high and firm, yet applied with TLC (tender, loving

care), grow up to be more mature, self-assured, and able to face the realities of life.

Good home rule serves as an anchor and point of reference for kids as they get older. Families that establish standards that are rooted in Christian-Judaic teaching have the greater advantage and likelihood of success, in that it is a morality that can be reinforced when the children go away from home and have contact with a Christian community elsewhere. Parents whose home standards are "homemade" or are only vaguely religious usually lose control over their children once they are away from home.

As I explain to the young residents in our Christian rehabilitation program, "The program here is Jesus. Therefore, when you graduate, the program will go with you everywhere you go." Parents who build their family life on the teachings and life of Jesus Christ are, in a sense, always united. They are linked by their common faith, common standards, and common truth.

6. **Be a "model" parent.** I believe one of the reasons for the rise in the number of kids turning to religious cults is because these organizations offer them group involvement, an authority figure, a caring community, and a sense of purpose and fulfillment—or, in a word, they are offered "a family." The Unification Church (the Moonies) in fact call themselves "The Family."

Studies have shown that kids who drift into cult groups were prime candidates because there was something missing in their own family life. Dad and Mom were missing— not literally, but emotionally, physically, and spiritually. Many of the cult kids had parents who were nonfunctioning. Business, a career, pursuing their own pleasures, and so forth, took them away from home, so they made up for it by giving their kids too much money and too much freedom—and not enough of themselves.

Children and young people need models. They need flesh-and-blood models who take the time to flesh out Christianity and demonstrate to their kids that they practice what they preach.

Among cult groups, the teaching has very little to do with attracting kids. It is the fact that someone took the time to develop a one-to-one relationship with them, the fact that someone took them in. At Jonestown, 900 people died for their "father."

Parents, your kids are going to belong somewhere, or to something, and they are going to find someone to model—somewhere or anywhere—if they don't find one at home.

7. **Don't try to be perfect.**   The number-one complaint of kids about parents is that they are hypocrites. It is dishonesty—not the failures of parents—that kids despise the most.

Parents who drink, use pills promiscuously, cheat or steal on a job, or are always trying to get around some law, then turn around and pounce on their kids for something they did wrong, soon lose the child's respect. This cover-up, or need to try to be perfect in the eyes of the child, is not possible or necessary. Young people do not mind adults making mistakes, as long as they are mature enough to acknowledge it when they make them. Anything less is hypocrisy, and such parents have no right to expect their kids to be any different from themselves. Many parents whose kids give them trouble are merely reaping the seeds the parents themselves have sown by their misdeeds.

Some other parents, especially religious ones, develop a very rigid life-style, in which they always try to live by the letter of the law. This is to be commended, but such rigidity can turn into legalism and result in a home where the parents are hard but not happy, tough but not tender, firm without feeling, and living under law without grace.

It is impossible to live perfect lives, and our children know it. The sooner parents show it, the more credibility and respect they will have from their kids.

8. **A family that "is together" has a better opportunity of staying together.**   One of the kindest comments one teenager can make to another is, "Boy, your family is really together." They are of course not just referring to physical togetherness, but to the emotional, philosophical, and spiritual unity that is a rarity nowadays.

I believe in the slogan "A family that prays together stays together." This points out, however, only one aspect of wholesome family life—the spiritual side. There is another side—the social side. An imbalance in either direction does more harm than good.

I can hear a mother or father saying, "All that sounds good, but my kid is beyond prevention. He is already smoking pot. What can I do?" The following is a list of simple but important recommended steps for parents who discover their teenager is using drugs. While the list is far from exhaustive, these at least are attempts to do the right thing in the right way.

1. **Know the signs that help to tell if your child is on drugs.**   Asking, "Can I know if my child is using drugs?"

is not unlike asking if you can tell if your child is awake or asleep. I am quite positive about this matter: Parents who are close to their kids, spend qualitative time with them, and have good personal relationships with them will know when something is wrong. When you really care about somebody, you know when something is bothering him.

Some of the early warning signals of a developing problem are:

Mood changes—a pleasant child may turn cynical, pessimistic, or moody.

Lowered energy level—may become restless, sleeping longer or at odd times, nervous, changing from aggressive to passive, apathetic.

Undependability—a normally helpful, attentive child may become forgetful, vague, and seem to be out of it.

Loss of self-confidence—the child may even feel oppressed—"somebody is out to get me"—having feelings of being persecuted or oppressed.

WARNING! These signs, in and of themselves, are not absolute evidence that your child is using drugs. They could symbolize a physical or emotional problem brought on by something else. But these are signs that something is wrong, and it is the duty of a parent to find out if that something could be drug abuse.

There are also other signs parents can pick up, such as: evading responsibility, attendance at school affected, disappearing at unusual times and for unusual lengths of time and with some unusual explanations, change in clothing style, a new and suspicious circle of friends, unusual odor in the teenager's room, the buying and burning of candles, and so forth.

2. **Don't overreact.**   Hearing your child is on dope may sound much worse than it is. In spite of fifteen years of greater public awareness of the drug problem, many parents do not really understand the difference between drug use, drug abuse, and drug addiction. To say that someone is "on drugs" or "using dope" may mean experimentation, or it could be regular use. And smoking pot is different from popping a pill and certainly vastly different from sniffing coke (cocaine) or injecting heroin into the vein.

"I feel the thing to do is to sit down and go through the old 'what, who, why, when, and where' type of thinking," states Dr. Edward R. Bloomquist in a pamphlet entitled *The Real Dope on Pot*. He continues, "The most important thing is for adults carefully, and I emphasize carefully, to take stock of the situation."

I believe there is a very short, yet vitally important, period, when a youngster begins experimenting with drugs, when the parent has the best opportunity to nip it in the bud. After this period (however long it may last), when the teenager gets deeper into drugs and the drug culture, it becomes increasingly difficult to get him (or her) to stop.

During this first discovery of drug use, avoid undue criticism, chastisement, or becoming so emotionally distraught that things are said in the heat of anger which are later regretted, as this can widen the gap between parent and teenager. This may drive his drug use underground or even push him deeper into it. Let parents panic inside— not outside. In the privacy of the bedroom, or when seeking counsel of a minister or trusted friend, is a time to let distress out. But when trying to get to the bottom of a child's drug taking, calmness and sanity with firmness are important. Dr. Bloomquist points out one other important result of a kid's drug use that can cause parents to lose their perspective in the matter and prevent proper reaction on their part. He states:

> Parents usually ask, "Where did I go wrong?" This is really not as pertinent as many people think. The "parent blamers" overlook the fact that in the majority of instances the parent couldn't have prevented his child from taking drugs. Today's youth are mobile, they readily intercommunicate, and most have a financial background that permits them to acquire and do almost anything they want.

A publication put out by the National Institute on Drug Abuse, entitled *Prevention Resources*, talked about a group of parents in Georgia who decided to take a stand against what they considered a cultural drift in their community that resulted in many of their children abusing marijuana. The pamphlet stated:

> . . . first shocked and disbelieving, the parents began facing the facts at home, and began looking beyond the family to see what was happening to their children. After going through the "guilt bag" they decided that if all their caring concern for their children, the comfortable, too-affluent life-styles, their education and professional backgrounds and values did not qualify them to assert themselves against a seeming consensus that marijuana is okay, they had better find out if their alarm was justified. . . . Instead of shaking their heads about the way things seemed, they began preparing to make changes. . . .

3. Don't ignore drug use. Some parents who understand the nature of their children's drug involvement may not be able to stop it, but they must not ignore it. Occasional pot smoking in some young people can quickly turn into regular, habitual smoking.

One mother said, "I was not only shocked to find my daughter was smoking pot, but she was doing it on a regular basis. Either she was very careful to hide the signs from me or I was very naive."

If kids are discrete, they can keep parents from knowing they are on pot for a long time. Some are even deceptive—living one life at home or church and another at school or with friends. However, once it is discovered, it is time to take action.

Taking action does not necessarily mean parents can get their children to stop smoking pot, although that is, or should be, the goal. The best parents can hope for is abstinence; the least is establishing a line of communication to help if the drug taking gets too far out of hand.

Maggie, the daughter of Susan Bromwell, writing in the article "How I Got My Daughter to Stop Smoking Pot," told her mother:

> Mom, except for one thing, you handled my pot problem just right. Parents should show their concern and should give their kids medical findings about pot. The thing you did wrong was to let me smoke in the house. You should have said, "I'm letting you make the decision as to whether you're going to smoke pot or not. But part of that decision is accepting the consequences—not only of the possibility of getting busted, but of what pot can do to you." If kids have

access to pot and they think its harmless—as most kids do—they're definitely going to get to abuse it. . . .

Of course, if it's younger kids who are doing the smoking, parents should insist they do not smoke, inside or outside the home, or disciplinary measures will be taken.

4. **Learn everything you can about the dangers of drugs.** The parents' group mentioned previously, called the De Kalb (GA) Families in Action, Inc. (DFIA), decided, "Instead of shaking their heads about the way things seem, they began preparing to make changes."

Among other things, they gathered a wide range of literature, going both to the "head shops," to see what their kids were reading, and to the library for the latest medical evidence. After their research, "They became more rather than less concerned about the effects of marijuana. They discovered that the information about marijuana most likely to fall into the hands of young people minimizes the dangers of marijuana as contrasted with alcohol. . . .

"The evidence they found was ample to assure them that marijuana was no innocuous weed or a sophisticated pacifier for children on the brink of, or in the midst of, their second most important developmental year, puberty."

5. **Try to mentally "detoxify" the drug user.** I use this term *detoxify* not in a physical sense, for marijuana does *not* physically addict anyone, but in a psychological sense. The parents, after careful reading and research on marijuana (as the De Kalb County, Georgia, group did), should take the right opportunity to mentally and psychologically detoxify their child's thinking about marijuana. I am convinced that, with the right information given in the right way to youth, many will make the right decision about

smoking pot. However, this must be done early, preferably before the youngster has even experimented.

6. **Join or organize parent-action groups to fight drug abuse in the schools and community.** Sadly, most schools, parent groups, and other civic organizations let down on their drug awareness after the LSD, heroin, and pill epidemic of the '60s and early '70s. During the past five to eight years, in the meantime, the decriminalization laws have gone into effect, and a nationwide discussion of possible legalization has created a whole new pot-smoking populace. Parents have done little to counteract this.

Hats off to the De Kalb, Georgia, parents, who felt the issue on drug abuse deeply enough:

> . . . to organize a campaign against apathy, ignorance, denial, and confusion in their neighborhood. After the parents began to check out the paraphernalia shops that had mushroomed in the metropolitan and suburban areas . . . questions led to actions, headlines, and before long, changes in the laws of Georgia governing the sale of drug-related objects to minors. . . . the organization can now take credit for making a sizeable impact on the consciousness of more than one state about the desirability of coming to terms with marijuana as a concomitant of adolescence.

If marijuana is decriminalized or legalized, it will only be because the lawmakers are responding to the voice or silence of the voters and the public at large.

Marsha Keith Schuchard, a founding member of the De Kalb Families in Action, has set forth some steps for concerned parents to follow in getting to the bottom of a local drug-abuse problem. Here is the list of what she has suggested:

Organize a group of committed and concerned parents who want to find out if there is a problem in the local schools and community—and to what extent.

Do something with the information you find. Don't just blame the kids, the school, or look for scapegoats. Be ready to confront parents of known users and suppliers with a motive to help, not hurt.

Work with local agencies that are credible and able to help.

Tell the kids at home what you are doing and why.

"Take a clear and firm stand *against any drug usage by your child.* . . . whatever your rule, make it clear and consistent."

Get all parents committed to enforcing prevention rules—and to punish violators.

Encourage frequent and lengthy home discussions between parents and kids.

Provide alternative activities for youth in the community.

Recognize that it will not be all sweetness and light. Kids who are cocooned into a drug-using peer group will fight to maintain that secure circle of friends. They can be sullen, defiant, deceptive, and downright dislikeable. A parent has to hang in there, to act out of pure faith, for a long time to make his or her child recognize her seriousness. This may take a few months or a few years. But, a parent owes it to the child. The alternatives are too hazardous. A child's drug usage can tear a family apart, but a parental and family struggle to regain a drug-free child can strengthen and reunify a family.

Provide for some on-going parent communication network to deal with any other problems that may arise among youth. It is easier to prevent than correct.

The above material and direct quotes were taken from Dr. Schuchard's speech to the South East Drug Conference, May 25, 1978, and published in the National Institute on Drug Abuse *Prevention Resources*, Winter 1978. Address: 5600 Fishers Lane, Room 10-A-56, Rockville, MD. 20857. Single copies are available at no cost. The address of De Kalb Families in Action is 1436 Cornell Rd. NE., Atlanta, GA 30303.

7. **Let your feelings be known to your state legislators.** If or when a bill comes up before your state legislators, send a letter to your local representative and let your concerns be known. If marijuana becomes legalized, we have no one to blame but ourselves.

8

The Courage to Say "No"!

IN THE GAME of football, there is an expression, "A good offense is a good defense." The team that keeps control of the ball offensively usually does not have to have its defensive team on the field a lot. This keeps the defense fresh and strong and better able to stop the other team's offense. In other words, control the football and you control the game. The chances of winning are better, then. The best "game plan" in life is to know how to control one's own body, mind, and soul—and thus control one's destiny. If not, other people and forces will gain control. Those who abuse their bodies and minds with drugs often have no offense in life. They have no goals, no purpose in life, little motivation, and no defense against the pressure from peers or other seductive forces within society. The Phillips translation of the Apostle Paul's writing to the Romans reads: ". . . Don't let the world around you squeeze you into its own mould . . ."(12:2).

How can the "squeezers" be resisted? How can young people find the courage and power to say no to drugs? There is what psychologists label a herd instinct in society, which young people especially fall prey to. This is the pressure to conform, to be and do what everyone else is doing. Everyone seems cut out of the same cookie cutter. Many find security in sameness. We are a nation of imitators. Many strive to be so different from their parents and the older generation, yet among peers, the pressure to conform is so powerful as to squeeze every ounce of individuality out of the younger generation. It is therefore a great challenge to help young people find both inner and outer resources to walk to the beat of a different drummer. How rare, but how refreshing, to find a young man or young lady today who has heeded the words of Solomon from Proverbs 1:10: "My son, if sinners entice thee, consent thou not."

It is possible to withstand the enticers and to keep from falling prey to all the destructive fads and fancies of a youth culture. I have seen the evidence in the lives of those who found the courage to say no and not experiment with pot in the first place. And I've seen those who did fall into the drug trap overcome their habit and addiction, to become clean and stay clean. In my work with addicted and troubled youth, I have seen literally thousands healed and rehabilitated from the horrors of hard-core narcotic addiction and drug abuse. I never cease to be amazed at their testimonies. The grace and power of God in transforming these social lepers is a modern-day miracle.

But equally exciting is to witness the faith and faithfulness of young people who never fall into the trap in the first place and who "walk not in the counsel of the ungodly, nor stand in the way of sinners, nor sit in the seat of the scornful" (*see* Psalms 1:1), the scornful being those who laughed and said, "Come on, what's wrong with smoking a joint?"

What does it take to keep pure and clean? Can our

children and youth find the intestinal fortitude and the willpower to say no to drugs? In spite of the fact that 40 to 50 million Americans have experimented with marijuana (the majority being under 25 years of age), it is also a fact that at least 50 percent or more of our youth do not smoke pot. True, the number of "tokers" is growing daily. However, millions have never experimented, and many who have, did not choose to make it a regular part of their lifestyle. Why didn't they? What causes some kids to go straight and others to smoke?

The following are a few helpful hints for young people wanting to find the courage to say no, so they "Don't copy the behavior and customs of this world, but be a new and different person with a fresh newness in all you do and think . . ." (Romans 12:2 LB). Because these suggestions are based on the teachings of the Bible, they are best understood and experienced and obtainable by those who have a personal relationship with Jesus Christ. However, the Bible contains good advice for every young person who is willing to listen. I have seen youth influenced by the teaching of the Bible even though they did not accept Christ into their lives. Of course good advice or good living will not help people get into heaven, but it may help them get along better on earth until they commit their lives fully to Jesus Christ. Here are some helpful hints in finding the courage to say no:

1. **Respect your body.** "I beseech you therefore, brethren, by the mercies of God, that ye present your bodies a living sacrifice, holy, acceptable unto God, which is your reasonable service" (Romans 12:1).

"What? know ye not that your body is the temple of the Holy Ghost which is in you, which ye have of God, and ye are not your own?" (1 Corinthians 6:19.)

Those who are God-fearing acknowledge there is a Supreme ownership of their bodies. The Bible teaches that we are His (God's) "off-spring"—"fearfully and wonderfully made." When we abuse the body, we abuse His body. Nowhere does it state in the Bible that we should not smoke cigarettes or pot. Yet many Christians believe it is wrong to smoke either, and, like myself, do not indulge in the drinking of alcoholic beverages. Where does this conviction come from? From the teaching contained in the above-quoted verses and others that are similar. We are to present acceptable bodies unto God. We are to live in our bodies as we act in a temple (church). We are to respect our bodies as we respect a temple—a holy place.

The argument some pot smokers use to justify their right to pollute their bodies is that they feel "It's my body, I can do with it whatever I please."

God says that it is not so. But even apart from this Christian teaching, I believe society has a right to expect the government to institute laws to protect youth from themselves—to not allow them to abuse their bodies. The right to use drugs violates the rights of others when we examine the effects marijuana has on automobile drivers, on the male sperm and the female reproductive organs (someone must protect the innocent children that could be born defective from a pot-smoking parent). I have a right to be assured that my auto mechanic, airplane-maintenance workers, and others responsible for delivering essential services are not stoned with pot when they are on the job.

I could make a long list of people who could violate my rights by being under the influence of marijuana on the job or when in daily contact with other people (my kids' schoolteacher, bus driver, subway conductor, nurse, physician, lifeguard, fireman, and so forth.) Just as I am entitled to sit in a nonsmoking section of an airplane or restaurant so I don't get cancer fumes blown in my face, so I am entitled not to have my human and social rights violated—either directly or indirectly—as the result of another person's altered perceptions, thinking, reasoning, or reactions while under the influence of marijuana. Another person's right ends where my safety and well-being begins, and it begins as soon as I step out of the door of my house.

If someone wants to smoke pot in the privacy of his own home or in some remote mountain cabin and inhale till his brain is saturated with the stuff, I have no right to deny him that privilege. But as soon as he steps into public territory and goes on the streets, or heads out onto the highway where I am driving, or reports to a job where I might have to go for his services, or enters a classroom with my son or daughter, or comes in contact with the human race in any way, shape, or form, he is responsible for respecting my rights, my lungs, my safety, my body, and my life.

I'm already paying a higher rate of taxes and insurance (auto and health) because of increased deaths, injury, and disease on the part of cigarette smokers and alcohol abusers; I don't want to have to pay an even higher rate as a result of the damage done in our society by the legalization of marijuana.

Apparently neither did a Long Island railroad employee.

A conductor on the Long Island Railroad had to leave his train because of a headache and nausea he got from what he termed the "pot train." His car of the train was filled with young people headed for a rock concert.

"I don't know whether it was marijuana, hashish, or something else," he said, "but the smoke was so thick you could hardly see one end of the car from the other," he stated, in an article entitled "LIRR 'Pot Train' Ticket Taker Is Feeling Punchy," which appeared in the New York *Post*.

He reported the situation to his supervisor and was told he should sign out sick, but he wouldn't do it, because he claimed he would lose three days' sick pay.

Both the laws of God and the laws of man teach us to have a healthy respect for our own bodies, as well as those of others.

2. **Keep your eyes on the goalposts.** A young football player became a born-again Christian. He was asked how he expected to keep from getting down or defeated in an atmosphere of cursing, dirty jokes, drinking, and carousing. The idea was also suggested to him that it might be best if he quit playing the game. He answered, "I know it's not going to be easy to live a Christian life—but I've already learned to keep my eyes on the goalposts and not look at the spiritual opposition when I come up to the scrimmage line of life. I look beyond the evil around me, to see Jesus. The Bible says, 'where your treasure is there will your heart be also.'"

He had learned that one of the secrets to success in life as a Christian is to set his affections on things above and not on the earth. Many youth are like the fellow who threw a dart on the wall, then went over and drew a circle around it. They aim at anything, and hit it every time. They do not live for tomorrow. They have set no goalposts before them. They don't know who they are, why they are, or where they're going.

For these drifters, smoking pot makes sense; they have nothing else to shoot for. They have no commitment to life, to a moral philosophy, religion, God, or even themselves. They are on a fast track to nowhere. Solomon, in Proverbs 1:31, describes what happens to the youth who has no goal and thus does whatever he wants: "That is why you must eat the bitter fruit of having your own way, and experience the full terrors of the pathway you have chosen" (LB).

The sad plight of the lost youth I observe is not just what they are, but what they are not. They sit on the sideline (or bleachers) of life and never get in the game. Talents are wasted, education dropped, energy drained, bodies abused, minds polluted. The waste of human potential among the physically and intellectually young is an appalling waste of our gross-national human product. I have witnessed the tragedy of young men whose bodies have become that of an older man, their emotions so stunted they never developed beyond adolescence, and with an education of a child, plus the wisdom of a fool. *Future* is not in their vocabulary. Their past is only a record in the courts. I weep for them. The media refer to some of them as the "throwaway generation." Either they have been thrown out by parents and society or they have chosen to throw away their lives themselves.

Thank God there is another silent but potent minority who have found through their faith in God that there is a "game plan" to life. They look to Christ and the Word of

God to give them the goalposts to aim for. They learn, for example, from Proverbs 4:23–27:

> Keep thy heart with all diligence; for out of it are the issues of life. Put away from thee a froward mouth, and perverse lips put far from thee [this includes putting a joint to the lips]. Let thine eyes look right on, and let thine eyelids look straight before thee. Ponder the path of thy feet, and let all thy ways be established. Turn not to the right hand nor to the left: remove thy foot from evil.

At the age of twelve, I knew what I wanted to be at the age of sixteen. At sixteen I knew where and what I wanted to be at eighteen. And at eighteen I knew what I wanted to do with my life at twenty-five. Since adolescence, I can never remember not having goalposts before me. Many was the occasion when the lure of the crowd and the temptation of the present loomed large before my eyes. But far ahead, as the above Proverb so simply states, I "let my eyelids look straight before me," and there were the goalposts. It made it easier to choose between present folly and future reward.

3. **Guard relationships.** Former pot smokers tell me the main thing that influenced them to experiment with drugs was pressure from friends. Peer pressure seems to be stronger today than with previous generations. The mass media also contribute to the philosophy of "everyone's doin' it." Movies, television, radio, and the music industry scream out to kids and influence their thinking and lifestyle. Parents very quickly become, in many cases, the secondary influence over their children's thinking and de-

cision making. Whether it be the lyrics of the latest hit tune or the slogan on a T-shirt, the message is the same: Turn on with sex, drugs, booze.

It is not drugs that kids want or fear the most: it's losing face among peers that is a fate worse than anything. To be "uncool" will cause a young person to make certain radical choices. If smoking pot or drinking is the initiation fee they have to pay to be accepted and respected by the street culture, they'll willingly pay the price. If "getting it on" gets them "in," then they are willing, ready, and able to participate.

"Kids turn on kids," said one young man, "not drugs, drink, or pushers." Therefore, it's not what kids have in common that brings them together, it's what they *do* in common. Relationships are often very shallow and superficial. It's not personalities coming together—it's bodies. It's not being together that counts, it's *doing* together.

It all gets boring quickly. Conversation has to be spiced with drugs or drink. Sex has to be boosted with a high. And the next time around, the joint may have to be more potent, the drug a little more powerful.

Youth who want to avoid drug abuse must avoid certain persons; they must guard their relationships. Friends must be chosen not only on the basis of who the person is, but who he hangs around. I told one young lady, who was about to begin a relationship with a certain young man, "Remember, when you accept Charlie, you're going to have to accept his friends. He may be okay on a one-to-one relationship with you, but you may also be buying a ticket into a crowd whose habits are not what you bargained for when you started dating Charlie."

A wrong relationship can lead to a wrong environment, which in turn can lead to a wrong decision. Anyone who wants to guard his behavior must first guard his relationships.

When choosing friends, it is wise to heed the instructions contained in the Proverbs 2:11–15 (NIV):

> Discretion will protect you,
>   and understanding will guard you.
> Wisdom will save you from the ways of wicked men,
>   from men whose words are perverse,
> who leave the straight paths
>   to walk in dark ways,
> who delight in doing wrong
>   and rejoice in the perverseness of evil,
> whose paths are crooked
>   and who are devious in their ways.

4. **A reason to say "No."** I understand why kids turn to pot. Something has to make them feel good. If the mind is not clean, if the body is not under subject of the spirit and soul of the person, if the heart is empty—artificial stimulants and mind-altering substances become necessary evils to provide temporary happiness and peace of mind. Now not all marijuana smokers are social dropouts or uncommitted individuals. Some smoke to escape the pressure of school, work, or just ordinary daily living. The fact that they have not found satisfaction from within themselves makes it necessary for them to go to some other source.

To be born again is to live life on a spiritual plane. Jesus promised believers that when He dwelt within them, "out of your inner most being shall flow rivers of living water."

In another place Jesus stated: "But whosoever drinketh of the water that I shall give him shall never thirst; but the water that I shall give him shall be in him a well of water springing up into everlasting life" (John 4:14). Some things add life, but Christ *is life*. Christians are motivated by a perpetual source of life—an eternal flame, to use another analogy—that need not be bought. They have a reason to say no. To the unbeliever, it is difficult to understand that Christians have a reason to avoid evil habits. A man who can eat steak will not eat dog food. A man who has experienced the supernatural high does not need the unnatural high.

"Those who let themselves be controlled by their lower natures live only to please themselves, but those who follow after the Holy Spirit find themselves doing those things that please God." Why? Because "Following after the Holy Spirit leads to life and peace [without drugs], but following after the old nature leads to death, because the old sinful nature within us is against God . . ." (Romans 8:5–7 LB).

In lower-nature living, it is as normal to smoke pot as it is for the spiritually minded to want to worship God. Christians do not keep away from sin and evil just because they are afraid of breaking commandments, although this is a part of the motivation. There is a higher reason for saying no. That reason is rooted in the love relationship with Jesus Christ. I love to hear former drug addicts sing these words by John Peterson: "I thirsted in the barren land of sin and shame, and nothing satisfying there I found, then one day to the cross of Jesus Christ I came, where thirsting spirits can be satisfied."

Those who have a reason to say no are the satisfied

customers. They have tasted and seen that the Lord is good. "It's the greatest high I've ever experienced," said one former drug abuser. I realize some may resent the use of the word *high* to describe the Christian experience, but we must remember that the new convert still relates his new-found joy to the vocabulary and life-style of his past. In this light, we should be able to appreciate that he is trying to say that Jesus Christ is so much greater and better than anything he experienced in the drug culture.

5. "No" Power!   A young Christian convert, with a past history of drug abuse, returned from his first visit to the old neighborhood since his new way of life. A broad smile crossed his face as he said, "I came face-to-face with my old friends. They didn't believe I had changed. They offered me my choice of pot, pills, booze, or coke [cocaine]—all free. I said no thanks. As I got ready to leave them, one hollered out, 'You'll be back—I bet.'

"I don't intend to. I said no for the first time in my life. It feels good to be free. Now I know it's true what I've read in the Bible—whom the Son [Jesus Christ] sets free, is free indeed."

This is the *no power*; that is, the power to refuse evil and do good, that I speak of. Many youth have all the reasons in the world, and in the world to come, to say no, yet they still give in to fleshly indulgences. Why? They lack the power to say no.

One of the main reasons youth—especially street kids—give for not accepting Christ is the fear of failure and phoniness. Many are so geared to failure they don't understand there is power available to them to be successful in the Christian way of life.

"This is the tremendous thing about coming to Christ," I explain to those hungry to receive the power to say no. "He doesn't call us to Himself without giving us what we need to be the Christian the Bible tells us we should be. He knows your past, your problems, your hang-ups, your record, your handicaps—He doesn't want you to fall or fail any more than you do. This is why the Bible says, '. . . as many as received him, to them gave he power to become the sons of God . . .'" (John 1:12).

Yes, power to *become*. The receiver becomes, among other things, a soldier instead of a slave. He attacks life, rather than retreating from it. He says no instead of yes to evil and wrong.

Examples of this no power or power to say no abound both in biblical history and all around us today.

Think of Moses. He refused to become the Pharaoh's yes-man. "It was by faith that Moses, when he grew up, refused to be treated as the grandson of the king, but chose to share ill-treatment with God's people instead of enjoying the fleeting pleasures of sin" (Hebrews 11:24, 25 LB). The key word is *refused*.

What about the handsome, well-dressed, robust young man named Joseph?

> One day at about this time Potiphar's wife began making eyes at Joseph, and suggested that he come and sleep with her.
>
> Joseph refused. "Look," he told her, "my master trusts me with everything in the entire household; he himself has no more authority here than I have! He has held back nothing from me except you yourself

because you are his wife. How can I do such a wicked
thing as this? It would be a great sin against God."

But she kept on with her suggestion day after day,
even though he refused to listen, and kept out of her
way as much as possible.

                                             Genesis 39:7–10 LB

No! No! No! Joseph made it loud and clear. So can the
Joes of today.

A yes to Christ is a no to the evil environment out of
which comes pot and other harmful habits.

The unsung heroes of our day—the superstars in the
eyes of the Lord—are those who have said no to drugs and
instead have said, "I'd rather have Jesus."